"Easy Reading Old World Literature"

Othello

LEVEL 5

Series Designer
Philip J. Solimene

Editor
Laura Algiere, M.Ed.

Cover Art by
Donald V. Lannon III

EDCON PUBLISHING

New York

Story Adapter
Rachel Armington

Author
William Shakespeare

Printed in U.S.A.
ISBN# 1-55576-337-5

CONTENTS

No.	TITLE	SYNOPSIS	PAGE
1	**A Perfect Soul**	Iago and Roderigo tell Desdemona's father she has run away with Othello. Othello agrees to meet the senators to face charges he used magic to win Desdemona.	6
2	**Which Report Is True?**	Desdemona tells her love for Othello. The council asks Othello to leave for Cyprus to fight the Turks.	12
3	**The Enemy in Cyprus**	A storm destroys the Turks before they reach Cyprus. Iago plans to deceive Othello into believing Cassio and Desdemona are in love.	18
4	**Honest Iago**	Iago tricks Cassio into losing his place as lieutenant. Iago persuades Cassio to ask Desdemona to help him get his position back.	24
5	**Chaos Comes Again**	Othello begins to believe Iago's hints that Desdemona and Cassio are in love. Desdemona asks Othello to give Cassio his position back.	30
6	**The Lost Token**	Desdemona loses the handkerchief Othello gave her when they were married. Iago hints that Desdemona gave the handkerchief to Cassio.	36
7	**A Heart of Stone**	Iago tricks Othello into thinking Cassio is boasting about Desdemona's love for Cassio when he is actually talking about another woman, Bianca.	42
8	**Whose Scheme Will Work?**	Othello won't listen when Emilia defends Desdemona. Iago convinces Roderigo that he must kill Cassio to win Desdemona's love.	48
9	**Murder in the Dark**	Roderigo attacks Cassio, but ends up being killed by Iago. As Othello leans over the sleeping Desdemona, he tells himself he will kill her in the name of justice.	54
10	**A Guilty Death**	Before Othello smothers Desdemona, she speaks to Emilia. Emilia tells Othello Iago fooled him. Othello kills himself to punish himself for his great sin.	60

About the Author

William Shakespeare was born in 1564. He lived in Stratford-on-Avon, a city in England. His mother's name was Mary Arden. His father, John, was a wealthy businessman. Very little is known about Shakespeare's early life. Some think he went to a free school near his home. There, children learned about God, studied Latin, and practiced speaking. When he was 18, Shakespeare married Anne Hathaway. They had a daughter and a set of twins.

Shakespeare moved to London. He was well-known as an actor. He also was famous for writing plays. He and his group of actors opened the Globe Theatre in 1599. They performed plays there in the summer. Later, they worked under King James I and were called "The King's Men." Then, they bought the Blackfriars Theatre for performing in winter. A fire destroyed the Globe in 1613. By the time a new Globe was built, Shakespeare had stopped writing. He died in his hometown of Stratford on April 23, 1616. No other writer's plays have been acted so many times, in so many countries.

Interdisciplinary Teaching Suggestions

Language Arts:
Create a Diary based on Shakespeare's Characters: Students must choose a character from the story. After reading each chapter, students should write a diary entry on their character's feelings based on the events in the story.
Interview Shakespeare's Characters: Break students up into pairs. Each student must choose a character from the story. Ask each student to write down five interview questions and interview each other.

Math:
Compare Prices: What was the average cost of food, shelter, and clothing? How were goods and services paid for in Shakespeare's time.
Create a Pie Chart: Research the population of London and the distribution of wealth during Shakespeare's time. Create a pie chart.

Science:
Scientific Discoveries During Shakespeare's Life: Galileo Galilei was born in the same year as William Shakespeare. Research and report on Galileo's discoveries throughout Shakespeare's life.

Social Studies:
Compare Lifestyles: In 1607, the first English settlement was established in Jamestown, VA. Research and compare life in Jamestown and life in London during Shakespeare's time. Create models of each society.

Geography:
Create a Map: Research and compare Europe in Shakespeare's time and today. Create a map of each.

General:
Create an Interdisciplinary Classroom Museum of Artifacts from Shakespeare's Story: Research, create, and detail the purpose and significance of each student's artifact in relation to the story.
Create a Classroom Bulletin Board: Break up students into small groups. Make each group responsible for an area of the bulletin board that pertains to the story. Create a story cluster describing literary elements from the story, for example setting, characters, and plot.

WORDS USED

Story 1	Story 2	Story 3	Story 4	Story 5
KEY WORDS				
bitter	confess	fleet	advice	deny
evil	duke	governor	drunk	dismiss
justice	noble	kneel	embarrass	distress
military	reputation	separate	generous	evidence
purse	slave	value	patience	monster
soul	witness	wit	pure	opportunity
NECESSARY WORDS				
betray	galley	approval	despise	chaos
deceive	marriage	courtesy	insult	conscience
ensign	passion	critical	mutiny	cuckold
hint	revenge	distract	reluctant	guilty
lieutenant	rumor		stab	
senator	suspicion			
villain				

Story 6	Story 7	Story 8	Story 9	Story 10
KEY WORDS				
confuse	civilized	behavior	instruct	crime
desire	memory	convince	resolution	failure
embroider	observe	fury	risk	mercy
innocent	plead	obedient	scorn	sacrifice
loyal	sin	relative	thrust	smother
visible	stun	scheme	weapon	sob
NECESSARY WORDS				
strawberry	gestures	curse	shroud	commit
swear	murder	false		fatal
token	strangle	misunderstand		suicide
torture	tempt	promotion		
trifle				
vow				

A Perfect Soul

PREPARATION

Key Words

bitter   (bit´ər)   unpleasant; hard to bear; causing pain
Jeff had <u>bitter</u> feelings toward Nina when she wouldn't go on another date with him.

evil   (ē´vəl)   1. causing harm; wicked
Harold invented an <u>evil</u> plan to get even with Karen.
2. wickedness
Juan wanted to protect his son from <u>evil</u> during the war.

justice   (jus´tis)   fair handling of the law
Even though Marcus was a stranger in the country, he hoped <u>justice</u> would free him.

military   (mil´ə ter´e)   of or about soldiers or war
When the enemy's navy arrived, the <u>military</u> forces trapped them in the harbor.

purse   (pėrs)   a small bag for holding money
The thief hid the stolen <u>purse</u> under his jacket.

soul   (sōl)   the spirit of a human being, where thoughts, feelings, and actions come from
Many people believe the <u>soul</u> is separate from the body and never dies.

A Perfect Soul

Necessary Words

betray	(bi trā´)	to turn against one's family or country *Jessie wouldn't <u>betray</u> her sister when she was asked who copied the notes.*
deceive	(di sēv´)	to trick someone so they don't see the truth *The hunter used a special whistle to <u>deceive</u> the ducks into flying near him.*
ensign	(en´sən)	a Navy officer of low position *As an <u>ensign</u> in the U.S. Navy, Lisa served under a lieutenant.*
hint	(hint)	to suggest a possible idea *Iris began to <u>hint</u> she should be the one to design the scenery for the play.*
lieutenant	(lü ten´ənt)	a person in the military position below a captain; someone who acts in place of his commander *While the captain was off the base, the <u>lieutenant</u> was in charge.*
senator	(sen´ə tər)	a person chosen to help rule a country for a period of time *In Venice, a man could become a <u>senator</u> if he were from a rich and respected family.*
villain	(vil´ən)	a very wicked person *Only a <u>villain</u> would pour poison into the stream.*

People

Moor a person from northwestern Africa. Moors are usually Muslims, who believe in one God and in the teachings of Muhammad.

Othello a great general, a Moor, and an older man. Othello is a person of color, like other Moors, but he is a Christian like the leaders of Venice. Christians believe in one God and in the teachings of Christ.

Places

Venice a city in Italy that ruled itself very peacefully for over a thousand years while trading with, protecting, and taking over many other lands.

A Perfect Soul

Iago and Roderigo argue outside Desdemona's home.

Preview: 1. Read the name of the story.
2. Look at the picture.
3. Read the sentence under the picture.
4. Read the first five paragraphs of the story.
5. Then answer the following question.

You learned from your preview that the Moor asked
_____ a. Iago to be his lieutenant.
_____ b. Iago to help him marry Desdemona.
_____ c. Cassio to be his lieutenant.
_____ d. Roderigo to marry Desdemona.

Turn to the Comprehension Check on page 10 for the right answer.

Now read the story.
Read on to find out how Iago betrays Othello.

A Perfect Soul

Two angry men walked through the dark streets of Venice. Everyone's doors and windows were locked. No one heard their bitter words.

"I never dreamed she would do this," stated Iago.

"But I paid you well to keep your eye on her!" complained Roderigo. "You've acted as if you own my purse, yet you didn't even warn me that she was falling in love! Why did you betray me?" Roderigo was so disappointed. He didn't even see where Iago was steering him. It was the house where Desdemona's father, the senator, lived.

"You said you hated the Moor," insisted Roderigo. He was upset. Iago had promised to win Desdemona for him.

"Three great men of Venice asked him to make me his lieutenant. But he chose Cassio!" Iago frowned. "Cassio doesn't have my military experience. I've fought next to the Moor in battle, and he has seen proof of my skill. But now Cassio is his lieutenant, and I am only his ensign."

"Leave him then," said Roderigo.

"We can't all be true leaders, and not all leaders can be truly followed," said Iago. "Smart men like myself deceive their leaders. They pretend to serve them, while really helping themselves. So, neither am I what I appear to be."

"The Moor will have a fortune!" Roderigo moaned at the thought.

"Tell her father about them," Iago suggested. "It will poison the happiness of that villain, the Moor."

Suddenly, Roderigo saw Desdemona's father's house. He shouted loudly, "Senator Brabantio!"

"Thieves! Watch your purse!" cried Iago even louder. An upstairs window opened; the senator leaned out. Hiding, Iago yelled, "You've been robbed. You've lost half your soul!"

Then Brabantio saw Roderigo. He called out impatiently, "I told you to stay away. Don't you realize how bitter I can make your life? Why shout? This is Venice, not the middle of nowhere!"

"Your daughter has run off with the Moor," said Iago.

Brabantio couldn't see Iago's face in the dark. "You are a villain," he shouted hotly.

"And you are a senator," said Iago. He didn't see much difference between the two.

"I know you, Roderigo," said Brabantio. "You'll answer for this!"

"Sir, I will answer anything. And I beg you to forgive us for disturbing you. You must already know your daughter has run away. But if you don't, you should not be angry with us for telling you. Why don't you check? If she is safe inside, let justice punish me for deceiving you."

Senator Brabantio's face wrinkled with worry. "I dreamed she would betray me."

"I can't be found here. I must still pretend to support the Moor as his ensign," whispered Iago to Roderigo. "Brabantio will be very angry when he finds her missing. It will be easy for you to lead him to the inn where the Moor is staying. I'll meet you there."

A moment later the door swung open and Brabantio cried out, "It is too true an evil; she is gone! My life will be spent in bitterness!" He grabbed Roderigo's arm. "Are they married yet?"

"I believe they are."

"I wish she had married you!" the father groaned.

Iago hurried to warn Othello. Outside the inn, the two men spoke. Iago accused Roderigo of lying about Othello's honor and upsetting the senator. "I wanted to kill Roderigo, but I'm not wicked enough to do evil deeds off the battlefield. Not even to help myself," whined Iago.

"It's better this way," said Othello.

"Are you already married?" asked Iago. "Brabantio is a man of power in Venice. He'll try everything to get Desdemona back home."

"My military services to Venice will silence his complaining," said Othello calmly. "And if boasting will help, I will boast. I will speak of the royal family into which I was born."

Lights moved toward them. "It's Brabantio," announced Iago. "Hide inside."

"I want to be found. My perfect soul will prove me right," replied Othello. "There is nothing wrong with my love for gentle Desdemona."

The lights came closer. Surprised, the two men recognized Cassio, Othello's newly named lieutenant, coming with other officers.

"Othello, the council wants you immediately. There is danger from the enemy," reported Cassio.

"I'll go with you quickly. Just let me spend a moment inside," replied Othello, as he slipped away.

Alone with Cassio, Iago took the chance to hint about Othello's secret. "The Moor has boarded a trading ship. If the law lets him keep his stolen goods, he'll be rich for life."

Cassio frowned. Iago made Othello sound like a pirate. "I don't understand," he said.

"He's married," explained Iago. Before Iago could say more, Othello returned. Then Cassio noticed Brabantio and his men hurrying toward them. The men on both sides of the street drew their swords. Iago pretended to be angry and waved his sword at Roderigo. "I'll fight with you!" Iago shouted.

Othello turned to Brabantio. "Senator, your strength is in your years of wisdom, not your sword."

"My daughter is beautiful and young. She has refused the best men of Venice. You are a thing to fear, not delight in!" Brabantio shouted. "Only magic would make her come with you. Therefore, I arrest you for practicing magic. To prison!" ordered Brabantio.

"I'll go willingly," said Othello, "but what should I tell these messengers who came to bring me to the council?"

"It's true," an officer told Brabantio. "The council sent for you, too. Current events hint of danger."

"Then bring the Moor to my fellow senators! They will feel this wrong as if it were against themselves. Without justice our country is nothing!"

9

A Perfect Soul

COMPREHENSION CHECK

Choose the best answer.

> **Preview Answer:**
> c. Cassio to be his lieutenant.

1. Iago and Roderigo never dreamed that Desdemona would marry
   ___a. Iago.
   ___b. Roderigo.
   ___c. the Moor, Othello.
   ___d. the senator.

2. When Iago says "men like myself deceive their leaders," he means he helps himself while he pretends to serve
   ___a. Roderigo.
   ___b. Othello.
   ___c. Brabantio.
   ___d. Desdemona.

3. Desdemona's father is
   ___a. Roderigo.
   ___b. Othello.
   ___c. Brabantio.
   ___d. Iago.

4. When Brabantio saw Roderigo outside his window he said,
   ___a. "Thieves!"
   ___b. "I told you to stay away."
   ___c. "And you are a senator."
   ___d. "Without justice our country is nothing."

5. When Brabantio realized Desdemona was gone, he wished that she had married
   ___a. Roderigo.
   ___b. Iago.
   ___c. Othello.
   ___d. Cassio.

6. Othello spoke with Brabantio
   ___a. while Roderigo woke Brabantio.
   ___b. before Desdemona left home.
   ___c. after Cassio arrived.
   ___d. while Iago argued with Roderigo.

7. Cassio asked Othello to meet with the council because
   ___a. they learned he was married.
   ___b. there was danger from the enemy.
   ___c. Brabantio needed a pirate.
   ___d. Iago wanted to fight Roderigo.

8. Who told Roderigo, Brabantio, and Cassio about Othello's marriage?
   ___a. Iago
   ___b. Othello
   ___c. Desdemona
   ___d. The senator

9. Another name for this story could be
   ___a. "Iago Begins an Evil Plan."
   ___b. "Desdemona Marries Roderigo."
   ___c. "Othello Betrays Cassio."
   ___d. "Iago's Perfect Soul."

10. This story is mainly about
    ___a. Desdemona's love for Roderigo.
    ___b. Iago's hate for Othello.
    ___c. Cassio's new military position.
    ___d. Othello's new fortune.

Check your answers with the key on page 67.

This page may be reproduced for classroom use.

A Perfect Soul

VOCABULARY CHECK

bitter	evil	justice	military	purse	soul

I. Sentences to Finish
Fill in the blank in each sentence with the correct key word from the box above.

1. Alison searched her _____ for the money to pay her grocery bill.

2. Michael joined the _____ , so he could be a soldier like his father.

3. The Halloween mask had an _____ grin and cruel eyes.

4. Many people believe that the _____ leaves the body at death.

5. The prisoner hoped for _____ from the judge.

6. Nathan felt disappointed and _____ about losing his job.

II. Word Search
All the words from the box above are hidden in the puzzle below. They may be written from left to right, up and down, or on an angle. As you find each word, put a circle around it. One word, that is not a key word, has been done for you.

```
B  J  U  E  K  B  S  S
B  U  E  B  L  L  O  O
V  S  V  B  B  U  L  U
B  T  I  T  I  E  D  L
M  I  L  I  T  A  R  Y
G  C  I  B  T  C  E  S
T  E  U  N  E  E  R  U
D  H  P  U  R  S  E  T
```

Check your answers with the key on page 69.

This page may be reproduced for classroom use.

Which Report Is True?

PREPARATION

Key Words

confess	(kən fes´)	to admit to doing something bad *No one would confess to eating the last piece of cake.*

confess (kən fes´) to admit to doing something bad
No one would confess to eating the last piece of cake.

duke (dük) a man of high birth who rules a small area of land
The wicked duke drove his brother out of the kingdom.

noble (nō´ bəl) 1. great because of birth into a high position
The private school only accepted children from noble families.
2. high and great in character
Their noble leader was the first to send aid to the starving citizens of the neighboring country.

reputation (rep´yə tā´shən) what other people think about a person's character
Evelyn had a reputation for changing her opinion from one day to the next.

slave (slāv) a person of any skin color, owned by another person and forced to serve them
A slave was often a prisoner of war, a person stolen from their home, or someone too poor to pay their debts.

witness (wit´nis) 1. to see or hear something happening
Yolanda felt upset to witness the accident.
2. a person who saw something happen, and later reports it in a court
Because Doug was a witness to the robbery, he agreed to explain the events, as they had happened, to the police.

Which Report Is True?

Necessary Words

galley   (gal´ē)   a long, narrow ship with oars, often rowed through the water by slaves
The Venice boatyard could build a complete galley in twenty-four hours.

marriage   (mar´ ij)   the condition of living together as husband and wife; married life
Monique and Pierre hoped for a long and happy marriage.

passion   (pash´ən)   1. very strong feeling
Yanni's music is full of passion.
2. very strong liking
Ever since Vincent saw his first horse, he had a passion for riding.

revenge   (ri venj´)   harm done in return for a wrong; returning evil for evil
Jenna decided revenge would only make things worse.

rumor   (rü´mər)   1. a story or statement talked of as news without any proof that it is true
If you hear a rumor that it will snow during summer vacation, don't believe it.
2. to spread information that may or may not be true
The students began to rumor that school would be closed because of the storm.

suspicion   (sə spish´ən)   a feeling, thought or idea that a person believes in
Michelle had a suspicion the boy was lying about stealing the candy, because she could smell chocolate on his breath.

People

Turks   a group of Muslims from Turkey, who took over many countries and who were still a strong force when Shakespeare wrote this play.

Places

Cyprus   an island that was very important to Venice's trade routes. The Turks won the island from Venice in 1571, during the war in the story of Othello.

Hell   according to Christians, a place where evil spirits live and where wicked persons are punished after death.

Which Report is True?

The council learns that the Turks have turned back to Cyprus.

Preview: 1. Read the name of the story.
                    2. Look at the picture.
                    3. Read the sentence under the picture.
                    4. Read the first five paragraphs of the story.
                    5. Then answer the following question.

You learned from your preview that the Duke asks Othello
_____ a. if he married Desdemona.
_____ b. for military help.
_____ c. if the reports are true.
_____ d. to find the missing Brabantio.

Turn to the Comprehension Check on page 16 for the right answer.

Now read the story.
Read on to find out how Desdemona fell in love with Othello.

Which Report Is True?

The council crowded around the dimly lit table. "Which report is true?" asked the Duke. "Since their first galley was sighted, each hour has brought a new rumor."

"My letters say one hundred and seven," said the first senator.

"And mine two hundred," said the second senator.

The next message rumored the Turks had turned around. The first senator shook his head. "The Turks want to deceive us. They need Cyprus, and they know the island does not have strong military protection." A new message proved his suspicion right. The Turks had gathered more galleys and turned back to Cyprus.

"Brave General, we need your help," said the Duke, when Othello came into the room. Then he noticed Brabantio. "We missed you tonight, noble Senator."

"I'm not here for the reports," said Brabantio. "It's my daughter! I can't think of anything else."

"Dead?" all the council asked.

"She's dead to me!" sighed Brabantio. "She's been stolen from me. How else could she have done something so opposite nature?"

"You decide how to punish the villain," said the Duke. "Even if it is my own son, I won't stand between you and justice."

Brabantio pointed to Othello. "Here's the man -- the same man you called to the council tonight, this Moor!"

"What do you say to defend yourself?" the Duke asked Othello.

"Say nothing," demanded Brabantio, "just confess!"

"Noble leaders, it is true. I have married his daughter. Since the age of seven I've lived in the military, so it's difficult for me to speak well about other ideas. But I'll try to explain how I won Desdemona," said Othello.

"My daughter is very shy and gentle. It's completely against her nature to fall in love with some-one she feared to look at. Why would she ruin her reputation in a marriage that isn't right according to nature? He must have deceived her with magic!"

"There is no proof. Did anyone witness his magic?" asked the Duke. No one replied.

"Let Desdemona answer," suggested Othello calmly. "And let her speak of me before her father."

The Duke agreed, and the Moor's ensign was sent to get her.

As they waited, Othello told how Brabantio often invited him to speak about his adventures. Desdemona would listen when she could get away from her chores. "I talked about my narrow escapes, how I was captured and sold as a slave. I spoke of my travels through strange lands with frightening creatures. One day, she hinted that she would fall in love with any man who could tell such adventures. So I took the hint. I told her I loved the way she listened. She showed so much wonder and feeling. The stories of my life, these are the only magic spells I used. Here comes Desdemona. Let her be my witness."

"This tale would win my daughter, too," said the Duke.

"If my daughter confesses these things are true, may I be struck down," Brabantio said. He turned to her, "In this noble company, do you know who it is your duty to obey?"

"I see here a divided duty. I owe you, noble father, for raising me; but I owe my husband the same duty my mother gave you. She chose you over her father, and so I choose Othello."

"It's better to let what has been stolen from you go freely," the Duke said to Brabantio.

"Would you let Cyprus go freely to the Turks? You accept their marriage because she isn't your daughter, but I feel differently," Brabantio said. "She is yours, Moor, because you've already taken her. I'm glad I have no other children. Because of your escape, Desdemona, I would be afraid to give them any freedom."

Immediately, the Duke turned to Othello, "You know how to defend Cyprus, and your reputation will give us support from the citizens. Meanwhile, Desdemona can stay with her father."

"I will not have it so!" stated Brabantio with passion.

"Nor I," said Othello.

"Nor I," said Desdemona. "Let me go with my husband."

Othello followed orders to leave for Cyprus that night. He put honest Iago in charge of Desdemona's travels to join him.

Brabantio left them with a bitter warning: "Watch her carefully, Moor. She deceived me; she may deceive you."

When all had left, Roderigo told Iago, "I'll drown myself. It's foolish to live; life is too painful."

Iago replied, "If you want to send yourself to hell, think of a better way than drowning. Trust me. She'll grow tired of his aging body, and his passion for her will change from sweet to bitter; so fill your purse and be ready! If you can make her betray her husband, we'll really get our revenge!"

Roderigo's passion for Desdemona was so great, he would even become a slave to win her. "I'll sell all my land," he decided.

That fool is my purse, Iago thought, as he watched him leave. So Iago planned revenge. He held the suspicion that his own wife had fallen in love with the Moor. Though it was only a suspicion, he treated it as if it were true. Now, Othello would suffer the same pain. Iago thought of handsome Cassio, the chosen lieutenant. *I'll deceive Othello into believing he's chasing Desdemona. Then I'll get my revenge twice -- against Othello and against Cassio, too!*

15

Which Report Is True?

COMPREHENSION CHECK

Choose the best answer.

1. Brabantio went to the council to ask for
   ___a. help fighting the Turks.
   ___b. justice against Othello.
   ___c. justice against Iago.
   ___d. help fighting Cyprus.

2. Brabantio asks Othello to confess to the council. In answer, Othello tells of his love for Desdemona. Then,
   ___a. Iago plans his revenge.
   ___b. Roderigo explains his love.
   ___c. Othello leaves for Cyprus.
   ___d. Desdemona explains her duty is to Othello, her chosen husband.

3. Desdemona fell in love with Othello because of his
   ___a. stories of danger and adventure.
   ___b. magic spells.
   ___c. noble family.
   ___d. galley.

4. The Duke wanted Othello to
   ___a. marry his daughter.
   ___b. live in Cyprus.
   ___c. help defend Cyprus.
   ___d. break off his marriage.

5. While Othello fights Cyprus, the Duke suggests Desdemona can stay with
   ___a. him.
   ___b. Iago.
   ___c. Roderigo.
   ___d. Brabantio.

6. Iago suggests Roderigo should
   ___a. help Desdemona travel to Cyprus.
   ___b. make Desdemona betray her husband.
   ___c. sell all his land.
   ___d. drown himself.

7. Iago plans his revenge: he will deceive Othello into believing that Desdemona is being chased by
   ___a. a senator.
   ___b. the Duke.
   ___c. Roderigo.
   ___d. Cassio.

8. Roderigo would do anything to
   ___a. go to Cyprus.
   ___b. be a Moor.
   ___c. be a senator.
   ___d. win Desdemona.

9. Another name for this story could be
   ___a. "Defending Their Love."
   ___b. "Brabantio Becomes a Senator."
   ___c. "Iago Becomes a Slave."
   ___d. "The Duke's Daughter Marries."

10. This story is mainly about
    ___a. Roderigo drowning.
    ___b. the Duke's daughter.
    ___c. Brabantio leaving for Cyprus.
    ___d. Othello and Desdemona defending their love for one another.

Check your answers with the key on page 67.

This page may be reproduced for classroom use.

Which Report Is True?

VOCABULARY CHECK

confess	duke	noble	reputation	slave	witness

I. Sentences to Finish
Fill in the blank in each sentence with the correct key word from the box above.

1. The police are looking for a _____ to the car accident.

2. The princess could only marry someone from a _____ family.

3. The teacher had a _____ for being a kind, caring person.

4. He has an ancestor who was sold as a _____ before the Civil War.

5. The police questioned the thief for seven hours before he would _____.

6. The _____ threw a grand ball for the visiting prince.

II. Matching
Write the letter of the correct meaning from Column B next to the key word in Column A.

Column A	Column B
____1. reputation	a. a man of high birth who rules a small area of land
____2. confess	b. great because of birth into a high position; high and great in character
____3. slave	c. to see or hear something happening; a person who sees something happen and later reports it in court
____4. duke	d. what other people think about a person's character
____5. witness	e. to admit to doing something bad
____6. noble	f. a person of any skin color who is owned by another person is and forced to serve

Check your answers with the key on page 69.

This page may be reproduced for classroom use.

The Enemy in Cyprus

PREPARATION

Key Words

fleet	(flēt)	a group of ships sailing together
		The girls made a <u>fleet</u> of paper boats to sail in the tub.
governor	(guv´ ər nər)	a person who rules over an area for his country
		The <u>governor</u> announced a new law to keep the rivers clean.
kneel	(nēl)	to go down on one or both knees, in a position of respect
		As King Harold raised his sword, he told the knight to <u>kneel</u> before him.
separate	(sep´ə rāt´)	1. to put or set apart
		The teacher decided to <u>separate</u> the twins because they kept fighting.
	(sep´ə rit´)	2. apart from others
		Remy and Mara sat at <u>separate</u> tables in the library.
value	(val´ yü)	to think or feel that something is important
		Anita began to <u>value</u> the glass necklace when she learned it had belonged to her aunt.
wit	(wit)	one's power to reason, learn or understand
		Sadie became respected for her <u>wit</u> after she earned perfect scores on all the tests.

The Enemy in Cyprus

Necessary Words

approval (ə prü´vəl) to have a good opinion of
Gary needed the committee's <u>approval</u> before he could begin the project.

courtesy (kėr´tə sē) politeness
Emma felt that treating customers with <u>courtesy</u> was better than being rude.

critical (krit´ə kəl) leaning towards finding fault
Angie was so <u>critical</u> of others, she had few friends.

distract (dis trakt´) to draw away the mind; to take away attention
The mother tried to <u>distract</u> the baby from crying by handing him a toy.

People

Emilia Iago's wife and Desdemona's servant

Montano a leader in Cyprus

The Enemy in Cyprus

As Desdemona came up the wharf, Cassio called,
"Men of Cyprus, kneel before this lady."

Preview: 1. Read the name of the story.
2. Look at the picture.
3. Read the sentence under the picture.
4. Read the first two paragraphs of the story.
5. Then answer the following question.

You learned from your preview that Montano is
_____ a. a leader in Cyprus.
_____ b. the enemy of Cyprus.
_____ c. the name of a harbor.
_____ d. the name of a ship.

Turn to the Comprehension Check on page 22 for the right answer.

Now read the story.
Read on to find out who will become the new governor of Cyprus.

The Enemy in Cyprus

The wind howled in Montano's ears. "Our walls have never before been shaken by such a blast!" he shouted. "The waves are terribly high. No ship could hold together in this storm!"

Montano, a leader in Cyprus, stood near the harbor. Other citizens joined him. They knew the Turks had sent a fleet of galleys to attack their island. Montano was waiting for any news that arriving ships might bring.

"Our war is done!" shouted a man running toward them. "Cassio, Othello's lieutenant, witnessed the drowning of most of the Turkish fleet! And Othello, himself, is on the way to be our new governor. He sailed on a separate ship, still out on the rough sea."

"Othello will make a worthy governor!" replied Montano with approval.

No sooner had Cassio joined Montano when they heard voices shouting, "A sail! A sail!" People ran to watch from a cliff, by the sea's edge. A cannon shot thundered. "They've fired a shot of courtesy," a gentleman told Cassio. "The ship is a friend to Cyprus."

It was Iago's galley. "His ship made good speed," Cassio said to Montano. "It's as if the high seas and howling winds sensed Desdemona's beauty and let her pass through to safety."

"Who is Desdemona?" asked Montano.

"She is now the captain of our great captain -- Othello's new wife," said Cassio. He explained that Desdemona had been left in Iago's care, while Othello rushed to Cyprus. As Desdemona came up the wharf, Cassio called, "Men of Cyprus, kneel before this lady."

"Thank you, brave Cassio," Desdemona said. "Please give me news of my husband."

"I haven't seen him since the storm forced our ships to separate," Cassio explained to a worried Desdemona.

Suddenly, another cannon shot was heard. "A sail! A sail!" someone cried.

"Go see who's coming into port," Cassio told one of the gentlemen of Cyprus. Then, welcoming Iago, Cassio turned to Emilia, Iago's wife. Greeting her with a kiss, he explained to Iago, "This is just my way of showing courtesy."

Iago didn't trust his wife, and he didn't like Cassio. "If my wife gave you as much of her lips as she gives me of her tongue, you would soon be tired of her," Iago joked.

Emilia looked so upset that Desdemona noticed right away. "Poor thing, you've hurt her feelings," Desdemona scolded Iago. "Now she can't talk."

"She talks too much!" insisted Iago. "At least when she's with you she has the wit to keep her critical thoughts to herself."

"You have no reason to say that!" Emilia protested.

Iago was quick to answer. "You women are silent when others are around, but you don't stop chattering at home. You'll pretend anything to get your own way!"

Desdemona smiled. "That's not true! You're teasing!"

"Oh, yes, it's true, or else I'm a villain," Iago answered.

"Do you value *anything* about women?" asked Desdemona. "What would you say about me?"

"I'm nothing but critical," Iago said. "It's better not to ask me."

Desdemona gazed past Iago at the people swarming over the wharf. The ragged sails of the newly arrived galley snapped in the wind. "This talk helps distract me from worrying about Othello. So, tell me, what sort of woman would meet with your approval?"

Iago sounded serious as he answered, "She would be beautiful, but not proud. She would be rich, but would not boast. If she were angry, she wouldn't take revenge. She would have great wit. She would be the best person there was..." He paused, pretending to be stuck.

"To do what?" interrupted Desdemona.

"The best person to raise children and run the house!" Iago laughed. He had cleverly avoided answering Desdemona's question.

"I expected your speech to have a more noble ending," she complained. "Emilia, don't learn the ways of your husband."

Cassio lightly touched Desdemona's hand. "You should value Iago as a soldier, not as a teacher!"

Noticing Cassio whispering to Desdemona, Iago smiled to himself with approval. *I'll tangle the great fly, Cassio, in his own web of courtesy!* he thought.

A trumpet announced Othello. Desdemona waited eagerly. "My soul's joy!" he exclaimed when he reached his wife. "What a calm after the storm! If I were to die now, I would die happy. My soul will never feel such joy again!"

"Of course it will. Our happiness will grow with our years together," Desdemona replied.

They sound beautiful together, thought Iago as they kissed, *but I'll soon knock them out of tune.*

Later, Iago tried to tell Roderigo that Desdemona and Cassio were in love. But he wouldn't believe it.

"Didn't you hear Cassio bid the citizens kneel before her? Didn't you see how he touched her?" Iago argued.

"That was only courtesy."

"Their lips were so close their breath joined," insisted Iago. "Cassio doesn't know you. Tonight, find a way to anger him so he strikes you. I'll arrange for some men to witness the fight. Then, they'll demand he be removed from his position."

Roderigo was grateful for Iago's advice. He agreed to do as Iago told him. Iago's plan became clearer with each step. Nothing could distract him from his passion for revenge.

21

The Enemy in Cyprus

COMPREHENSION CHECK

Choose the best answer.

1. Cassio witnessed the
   ___a. drowning of much of the Turkish fleet.
   ___b. drowning of Montano.
   ___c. fleet of galleys taking over Cyprus.
   ___d. drowning of Othello.

2. Who was coming to fill the position of governor of Cyprus?
   ___a. Cassio
   ___b. Othello
   ___c. Iago
   ___d. Desdemona

3. Cassio joined Montano. Iago's galley arrived with Desdemona. Then,
   ___a. the storm came.
   ___b. the Turkish fleet went down.
   ___c. the storm separated Venice's fleet.
   ___d. a trumpet announced Othello's arrival.

4. Iago
   ___a. did not trust Emilia.
   ___b. liked Cassio.
   ___c. arrived after Othello.
   ___d. kissed Emilia.

5. Who is the *real* "Enemy in Cyprus"?
   ___a. The Turks
   ___b. Montano
   ___c. Roderigo
   ___d. Iago

6. When Iago tells Desdemona what sort of a woman is worthy of approval,
   ___a. he's talking about his mother.
   ___b. Emilia protests against Iago.
   ___c. Desdemona is disappointed with his answer.
   ___d. Cassio does not listen to Iago.

7. The "web of courtesy" that Iago will use to catch Cassio means
   ___a. Cassio's telling Desdemona to value Iago as a soldier, not as a teacher.
   ___b. Cassio's worrying about Othello.
   ___c. Casssio's politeness towards Desdemona.
   ___d. Cassio's telling Montano that Othello will be governor.

8. Iago deceives Roderigo into believing Cassio and Desdemona are in love, and asks him to
   ___a. drown Othello.
   ___b. fight Montano.
   ___c. drown Desdemona.
   ___d. fight Cassio.

9. Another name for this story could be
   ___a. "Cassio Loves Emilia."
   ___b. "Othello Becomes Governor."
   ___c. "Iago, the Fly."
   ___d. "Othello is Late."

10. This story is mainly about
    ___a. Iago deceiving the others.
    ___b. Desdemona's love for Cassio.
    ___c. Emilia's talking too much.
    ___d. Cassio's falling in love with Emilia.

Check your answers with the key on page 67.

The Enemy in Cyprus

VOCABULARY CHECK

fleet	governor	kneel	separate	value	wit

I. Sentences to Finish
Fill in the blank in each sentence with the correct key word from the box above.

1. The _____ of ships prepared for battle against the enemy.

2. We had to _____ the boys because they kept fighting.

3. Her quick _____ made learning a second language easy.

4. My parents made us work after school to teach us the _____ of a dollar.

5. Hoping to get more votes, the _____ toured the state before the big election.

6. When I was little, I would _____ by the side of my bed and say my prayers.

II. Word Use
Put a check next to YES if the sentence makes sense. Put a check next to NO if the sentence does not make sense.

1. When asked to **kneel**, you must stand straight and tall. _____Yes _____No

2. The **governor** worked hard for the people in his state. _____Yes _____No

3. The **fleet** of fishing boats returned safely back to the harbor _____Yes _____No
   when they heard about the approaching storm.

4. To **separate** things properly, you must put everything away . _____Yes _____No

5. Because of her great **wit**, Nadia made everyone cry. _____Yes _____No

6. It is wise to take good care of something you really **value**, _____Yes _____No
   so it will last a long time.

Check your answers with the key on page 69.

This page may be reproduced for classroom use.

Honest Iago

PREPARATION

Key Words

advice   (ad vīs´)   an opinion about what should be done
The gardening book gave advice on how to choose the best roses.

drunk   (drungk)   out of control of one's mind and body from drinking too much
When Mark's friends realized he was drunk, they decided to walk him home.

embarrass   (em bar´əs)   to make someone feel ashamed or awkward
Laurie didn't want to embarrass Nina by repeating the rumors she had heard.

generous   (jen´ər əs)   1. willing to share with others; unselfish
The neighbors were very generous to the family whose house burned down.
2. noble and forgiving; not mean
Elsa was generous to forgive me after I ruined her favorite sweater.

patience   (pa´ shəns)   willingness to put up with waiting, pain, trouble, etc.
The teacher kept his patience and waited until all the students were quiet.

pure   (pyür)   1. perfect; without fault; without evil
A person with a pure heart loves without expecting anything in return.
2. not mixed with anything else
Gemma's bracelet is made of pure gold.

Honest Iago

Necessary Words

despise   (di spīz´)   to have a strong feeling against
Elaine knew Karen would <u>despise</u> the green sweater, but she gave it to her as a joke anyway.

insult   (in sult´)   to say or do something very rude to
Franklin didn't mean to <u>insult</u> the cook when he said the meat needed more sauce.

mutiny   (mūt´n ē)   taking of power from a commander by soldiers or sailors
During the <u>mutiny</u>, the men locked their captain below the ship's deck.

reluctant   (ri luk´tənt)   unwilling or not wanting to; slow to act because unwilling
The cat was <u>reluctant</u> to step on the wet grass.

stab   (stab)   to wound with something sharp and pointed
When the robber attacked him from behind, Scott grabbed a pen to <u>stab</u> him.

Honest Iago

The people feast to celebrate Othello's marriage and being saved from war.

Preview: 1. Read the name of the story.
2. Look at the picture.
3. Read the sentence under the picture.
4. Read the first paragraph of the story.
5. Then answer the following question.

You learned from your preview that Othello celebrated his
marriage   _____ a. by giving a feast to the Turks.
_____ b. by giving a feast for all of Cyprus.
_____ c. by drowning the enemy.
_____ d. by telling his men to be generous.

Turn to the Comprehension Check on page 28 for the right answer.

Now read the story.
Read on to find out what happens while the people of Cyprus celebrate.

Honest Iago

To celebrate his marriage and the drowning of the enemy, Othello offered a feast. The people of Cyprus could eat and drink all they wanted that night. Othello was generous to the citizens. But he ordered his own men to control themselves.

Iago seemed reluctant to go on watch duty with Cassio. "It's only ten o'clock," he fussed. "The Moor sent us away early. He wants to be with his wife. She's very inviting."

"She has a pure heart," said Cassio.

"Her eyes ask for love," replied Iago.

"She is a noble lady," insisted the polite Cassio.

Cassio would not insult Desdemona's reputation. So, Iago tried a different approach. "Some gentlemen are coming to drink to the General's health."

"I already drank some wine mixed with water tonight," Cassio said. "Pure wine changes me. I don't dare drink more now."

Iago insisted that Cassio invite the men for a drink. He had already made certain Montano and his men were drunk. By the time Cassio came back with them, he was drunk too. Iago was glad his patience was paying off. He sang high-spirited songs to encourage Cassio to drink more.

"A perfect song!" said Cassio.

"Do you want to hear it again?" asked Iago.

"No. I must remember that I hold a position of respect and honor," said Cassio. "God saves some souls, and some souls are lost. I hope to be saved."

"So do I," said Iago.

"Patience, Iago! The lieutenant comes before the ensign, so I must be saved before you!" As Cassio laughed at his own joke, he didn't realize he had insulted Iago. Iago's eyes flashed with anger.

"Cassio's love of wine is dangerous for the island," Iago whispered to Montano, as Cassio staggered in. "You should tell the noble Moor about Cassio," Montano said.

Iago saw Roderigo slip into the room. He waved to Roderigo to follow Cassio. Iago pretended to refuse Montano's advice. "I love Cassio too much to tell the Moor. But, listen, what is that noise?"

"Help! Help!" The cries grew louder. Suddenly, Cassio chased Roderigo into the room and tried to stab him. Montano stepped between them, only to have Cassio turn on him.

Iago shoved Roderigo out the door. "Run, and yell that there is a mutiny." Then Iago fluttered around Montano and Cassio. "Stop, oh stop! The alarm bells are ringing. The whole town will think there's a mutiny. Lieutenant, you'll embarrass yourself!"

Montano was bleeding when Othello rushed into the room. "I am stabbed! He dies too!" Montano shouted, as he attacked Cassio again.

"Have we become the enemy Turks?" demanded Othello. "Did God drown our enemy just so we could kill each other instead? How did this start?"

Iago hesitated, as if reluctant to place blame. "I don't know how this quarrel started." Cassio refused to explain the fight as well. And Montano would only say that he had been defending himself.

"I am losing patience!" Othello shouted. "You men are fighting each other instead of protecting the town! Iago, who began it?"

"I'd rather cut out my own tongue than harm Cassio. But the truth will not hurt him," said Iago. So he told how Cassio had first chased in a stranger and then attacked Montano, when he had tried to separate them. "Sometimes even the best men forget self-control," Iago said generously. "I'm sure the stranger had insulted Cassio somehow."

"Iago, I know you are trying to lessen his blame," said Othello. "But, Cassio, you are no longer my officer." Then, Othello led Montano out to take care of him.

Cassio groaned. "Are you hurt?" asked Iago.

"My reputation is ruined!" cried Cassio. "I have lost the undying part of my human nature. Now, I am only an animal!"

"Reputation has no true meaning," scolded Iago. "It's given without reason and lost without fault. You can win the General back."

"I am too embarrassed. He has every reason to despise me."

"Who was that stranger you were chasing?" asked Iago.

"I don't know." said Cassio. "Why did I get myself drunk? We men put an enemy in our mouths that steals away our brains!"

"Our General is ruled by his wife now," said Iago. "Confess your faults to her. The generous lady will give you more help than you ask for. Believe my love and honest kindness. I insist you try."

Who could ever call me a villain? thought Iago. *My advice really is a good way for Cassio to win back his position. Desdemona is a generous person. The Moor will surely respect her wishes. And my advice is the same as if I honestly wanted to help Cassio.* Iago chuckled to himself. *While she begs her husband to take back Cassio, I'll poison the Moor's thinking. I'll tell the Moor she now despises him for love of Cassio. Her own pure heart will weave the net to trap them all!*

Roderigo arrived, complaining, "My purse is empty. I've been beaten up. All I've received for my pain is experience! So, with no money, and a little more wit, I will return to Venice."

"You have no patience! Don't you realize you've knocked Cassio from his position? And you were hardly scratched." Iago turned to watch the warm glow of dawn spread over the harbor. "Get some sleep. I'll tell you more later. Now is the time for me to act quickly."

Honest Iago

COMPREHENSION CHECK

Preview Answer:
b. by giving a feast for all of Cyprus.

Choose the best answer.

1. First, Iago tried to get Cassio to insult Desdemona, then he tried to get Cassio
   ___a. to stab Montano.
   ___b. drunk.
   ___c. to fight with him.
   ___d. to stab Roderigo.

2. While Cassio laughed at his own joke, Iago
   ___a. laughed with Cassio.
   ___b. told the joke to Montano.
   ___c. was patient.
   ___d. became angry, because it reminded him that Cassio had a higher rank.

3. Iago told Montano that Cassio was drunk, because he wanted
   ___a. to protect Montano.
   ___b. someone to take care of Cassio.
   ___c. to protect Othello.
   ___d. to make himself look good.

4. Who was shouting for help?
   ___a. Iago
   ___b. Othello
   ___c. Roderigo
   ___d. Cassio

5. When Iago finally explains how the fight began, Othello believes that
   ___a. Iago is protecting Cassio.
   ___b. Iago is deceiving everyone.
   ___c. Montano is deceiving everyone.
   ___d. Roderigo is deceiving everyone.

6. Who is no longer Othello's officer?
   ___a. Montano
   ___b. Cassio
   ___c. Roderigo
   ___d. Iago

7. After losing his position, Cassio blames
   ___a. Iago.
   ___b. Othello.
   ___c. Roderigo.
   ___d. himself for drinking too much.

8. Iago tells Cassio to talk to _____ about getting his position back.
   ___a. Desdemona
   ___b. Montano
   ___c. Othello
   ___d. Roderigo

9. Another name for this story could be
   ___a. "The Turkish Feast."
   ___b. "Self-Control."
   ___c. "Roderigo Bleeds."
   ___d. "Cassio Ruins his Reputation."

10. This story is mainly about
   ___a. Cassio losing his position with help from Iago.
   ___b. a celebration.
   ___c. having patience.
   ___d. Othello's ruined reputation.

Check your answers with the key on page 67.

Honest Iago

VOCABULARY CHECK

advice	drunk	embarrass	generous	patience	pure

I. Sentences to Finish
Fill in the blank in each sentence with the correct key word from the box above.

1. My sister didn't want to _____ me with her silly jokes.

2. The secret to my aunt's pancakes is _____ maple syrup from Vermont.

3. Paul had to call the police because his neighbor was _____ and out of control.

4. When my father lost his _____ after just one lesson, he sent my brother to driving school.

5. The best _____ for good health is to avoid smoking.

6. Our teacher is so _____ with his time, that he will stay late or come early to school if we need help.

II. Using the Words
On the lines below, write six of your own sentences using the key words from the box above. Use each word once, drawing a line under the key word.

1. _____

2. _____

3. _____

4. _____

5. _____

6. _____

Check your answers with the key on page 70.

This page may be reproduced for classroom use.

Chaos Comes Again

PREPARATION

Key Words

deny (di nī´) refuse
The farmer had the right to deny traffic across his fields.

dismiss (dis mis´)
1. send away
Why did your teacher dismiss your class early?
2. put out of mind; stop thinking about
Sandra tried to dismiss the awful dream and think happy thoughts.

distress (dis tres´) great pain or sorrow; trouble
Roberta felt deep distress when her boyfriend was called for military service.

evidence (ev´ə dəns) facts; proof; anything that shows what is true and what is not true
What we thought was evidence of a killing was really red food coloring on the floor.

monster (mon´stər) a horrifying creature of the imagination; a person too wicked to be human
Only a monster could do such a dreadful deed!

opportunity (op´ər tü´nə tē) a good chance
When the passenger next to her mentioned he was hungry, Frances took the opportunity to sell her daughter's Scout cookies.

Chaos Comes Again

Necessary Words

chaos   (kā´os)   complete loss of order
Henry's sudden death put his family's life into <u>chaos</u>.

conscience   (kon´shəns)   a sense of right and wrong; ideas and feelings within you that tell you when you are doing right, and warn you of what is wrong
Irving's <u>conscience</u> told him to phone for help when he saw the accident, and so he did.

cuckold   (kək´əld)   a man whose wife is not faithful to him
Long ago, a man would be called a <u>cuckold</u> if his wife betrayed him for another lover.

guilty   (gil´tē)   having done wrong; deserving blame
The detective was <u>guilty</u> of lying when he wouldn't give all the information to the police.

Chaos Comes Again

Cassio hires musicians to play music for Othello and his wife.

Preview:
1. Read the name of the story.
2. Look at the picture.
3. Read the sentence under the picture.
4. Read the first two paragraphs of the story.
5. Then answer the following question.

You learned from your preview that Cassio hopes to
_____ a. play music for Emilia.
_____ b. cause Othello distress.
_____ c. speak with Emilia's mistress.
_____ d. dismiss the Moor's servant.

Turn to the Comprehension Check on page 34 for the right answer.

Now read the story.
Read on to find out if Desdemona will speak in Cassio's favor.

Chaos Comes Again

Cassio hoped to win back Othello's favor. So, he brought musicians to play beneath the newly married couple's window. But the Moor's servant rushed out to dismiss them. "Your music causes distress. The General begs you to stop the noise. So pack up and leave!"

Next, Cassio paid the servant to find Emilia. "Ask if I may speak with her," Cassio said. He hoped Emilia would bring him to her mistress. Meanwhile, Iago arrived. He offered to distract the Moor for Cassio. Then, he could meet alone with Desdemona.

Soon, Emilia led Cassio through the garden. She told him her lady was already speaking in his favor. "The General told his wife he will take you back as soon as an opportunity appears."

"Bring me to her," begged Cassio. When they found Desdemona, he poured out his distress.

Desdemona told him, "Be certain, good Cassio, I will do all I can. Do not doubt it. You and my lord will be as friendly again as you were before."

"Look, here come Iago and Othello," reported Emilia.

"Stay and hear me speak for you," urged Desdemona.

Cassio shook his head nervously. "I'd make things worse."

Iago wanted the Moor to see Cassio leaving the garden. "Ha, I don't like that!" Iago said, just loudly enough to be heard.

Othello followed the direction of Iago's gaze. "Was that Cassio with my wife?" he asked.

Iago pretended to dismiss the idea. "Cassio wouldn't sneak away from you as if he were guilty of something."

"I do believe that was Cassio," said Othello.

When Othello stepped up to her, Desdemona spoke. "My lord, I was just with a man who suffers greatly from losing your favor."

Othello pretended not to understand. "Who do you mean?"

"Your lieutenant, Cassio!" said Desdemona. "He is truly sorry for his mistake. Won't you call him back?"

"Not now," answered Othello.

"If *you* were to ask *me* a favor, I would not deny you," she said. "He's the same man you brought when you were courting for my hand in marriage. He defended you whenever I saw your faults."

Hearing this, Iago's sharp mind began weaving a new thread into the web.

Othello agreed he would see Cassio. "I'll never deny you anything," he promised Desdemona. As he watched her leave with Emilia, his suspicion melted away. "My soul would be in chaos again without her love."

"I was surprised to learn that Cassio knew Desdemona in Venice," Iago said.

"He often took messages between us," Othello said. "He is an honest man."

"Honest, my lord?"

"Yes, honest," said Othello. "What do you think?"

"Think, my lord?"

"You repeat what I say as if some monster in your thoughts were too terrible to be shown!" said Othello. "Tell me!"

"A slave is free to keep his thoughts to himself, and so am I," said Iago. "What if my thoughts are wild and false? False thoughts enter even the purest hearts. They argue with honest thoughts as if they sit together in a court of law."

"If you are my friend," said Othello, "you must tell me if you think someone betrayed me."

"My jealousy often shapes faults that aren't there," Iago said. "Your nature wouldn't suspect evil in people as mine does."

"What do you mean?"

"The reputation of a man and a woman," said Iago, "is the jewel of their souls. If someone steals my purse, they steal nothing. But he who robs me of my reputation makes me poor indeed."

"By heaven, tell me your thoughts!" demanded Othello.

"Oh, beware of jealousy! It is a green-eyed monster that fools the very heart it feeds on," said Iago. "If a cuckold doesn't love his wife, he can still be happy after he learns she has betrayed him. However, if a man really loves his wife, but is never sure if she is faithful, he suffers every minute. He always wonders if he is a cuckold."

"My wife is lovely, gifted and popular. That's no reason for me to be jealous," Othello replied. "She chose me freely to be her husband. No, Iago, I must have hard evidence before I doubt her."

"I won't talk about evidence. Not yet...," said Iago. "Watch her with Cassio. You don't know about women from Venice like I do. Their conscience tells them it's all right to do evil, as long as no one finds out. Remember, she did deceive her father."

Brabantio's voice echoed in Othello's mind. "I think Desdemona is honest," he said. But he didn't sound so sure of himself.

"I hope you think so for a long time," answered Iago.

"Yes," mumbled the Moor, "yet our nature has its weaknesses."

Iago seized this opportunity to repeat Brabantio's warning. "This marriage goes against nature." He continued, "It's strange how she turned away men from her own country, of her own color, and her same noble life. One might suspect such a woman to have a weak conscience. Of course, I'm not saying that about *your* wife. But she may realize what she has done, and wish she had never married."

Othello's mind was in chaos. *Why did I marry?* he wondered. Iago was winning his case. Othello now suspected she was guilty. He wasn't even giving her the opportunity to defend herself.

Chaos Comes Again

COMPREHENSION CHECK

Choose the best answer.

1. Desdemona promised Cassio that she would
    ___a. leave Othello.
    ___b. marry Iago.
    ___c. talk to Emilia for him.
    ___d. talk to Othello for him.

2. Who wanted the Moor to see Cassio leaving the garden?
    ___a. Othello
    ___b. Desdemona
    ___c. Iago
    ___d. Emilia

3. To whom does Desdemona say, "You and my lord will be as friendly again as you were before"?
    ___a. Othello
    ___b. Iago
    ___c. Roderigo
    ___d. Cassio

4. Who had defended Othello whenever Desdemona had seen his faults?
    ___a. Brabantio
    ___b. Iago
    ___c. Roderigo
    ___d. Cassio

5. First, Desdemona said she would help Cassio. Then, she spoke to Othello. Then,
    ___a. Iago began to develop a new plan.
    ___b. Othello agreed to see Iago.
    ___c. Emilia left with Cassio.
    ___d. Cassio agreed to meet Othello.

6. Who was surprised to learn that Cassio had known Desdemona in Venice?
    ___a. Othello
    ___b. Iago
    ___c. Roderigo
    ___d. Emilia

7. The green-eyed monster Iago describes is
    ___a. happiness.
    ___b. sadness.
    ___c. jealousy.
    ___d. anger.

8. The green-eyed monster "fools the very heart it feeds on." In this story *that heart* belongs to
    ___a. Iago
    ___b. Othello
    ___c. Desdemona
    ___d. Cassio

9. Another name for this story could be
    ___a. "A Cuckold Loves His Wife."
    ___b. "Cassio in Command Again."
    ___c. "Iago Weaves a New Web."
    ___d. "Othello's Suspicion Melts Away."

10. This story is mainly about
    ___a. Iago's planting jealous thoughts in Othello's mind.
    ___b. musicians playing for Othello.
    ___c. Cassio's meeting with Iago.
    ___d. Othello's wondering why he married Desdemona.

Check your answers with the key on page 67.

This page may be reproduced for classroom use.

Chaos Comes Again

VOCABULARY CHECK

| deny | dismiss | distress | evidence | monster | opportunity |

I. Sentences to Finish

Fill in the blank in each sentence with the correct key word from the box above.

1. Many people describe jealousy as "the green-eyed _____."

2. Sean did not _____ his brother anything while Pearse was sick.

3. Many people succeed when given the _____ of a good education.

4. During the attack on their country, the citizens were in _____.

5. The police searched the suspect's home looking for _____ .

6. Abe tried to _____ the rumors about Dan from his mind.

II. Crossword Puzzle. Use the words from the box above to fill in the puzzle. Use the meanings below to help you choose the right answer.

ACROSS
1. send away; stop thinking about
3. a good chance
4. trouble; great pain
5. facts; proof

DOWN
1. refuse
2. a horrifying creature of the imagination; a person too wicked to be human

Check your answers with the key on page 70.

This page may be reproduced for classroom use.

35

The Lost Token

PREPARATION

Key Words

confuse (kən fyüz´)
1. to disturb someone's thinking so that nothing is certain;
*"If you lie to young children, you will confuse them,"
the teacher warned.*
2. to mix up
"These directions confuse me!" exclaimed Ed.

desire (di zīr´)
to wish for or long for earnestly
*Lucy signed up for lessons because of her strong
desire to learn how to drive.*

embroider (em broi´ dər)
to sew designs onto cloth
*My grandmother used to embroider colorful designs
on tablecloths and napkins.*

innocent (in´ ə sənt)
not guilty; doing no wrong or evil; free from wrong
*Even though the judge accused her of lying, Courtney
knew that she was innocent.*

loyal (loi´ əl)
true and faithful to someone or something
*The country remained loyal to the president when the
enemy took over his government.*

visible (viz´ə bəl)
able to be seen
*As light struck the diamond, bands of color became
visible.*

The Lost Token

Necessary Words

strawberry	(strô´ ber´ ē)	a small, bumpy, juicy red fruit that grows close to the ground *Kim picked a <u>strawberry</u> to put on top of her ice cream.*
swear	(swâr)	1. to use bad language *Tony's girlfriend asked him not to <u>swear</u> when they were together.* 2. to promise *A witness at a trial is asked, "Do you <u>swear</u> to tell the truth, the whole truth, and nothing but the truth?"*
token	(tō´ kən)	a mark or sign of something *The mayor gave his visitor a silver pen as a <u>token</u> of friendship.*
torture	(tôr´ chər)	1. the act of causing great pain to a person or animal *Some governments use <u>torture</u> to force innocent citizens to confess.* 2. to cause very great pain to *"How can anyone <u>torture</u> another person!" exclaimed Diane when she read the news article.*
trifle	(trī´ fəl)	a thing of little value; something that is not very important *The smallest <u>trifle</u> can delight a young child.*
vow	(vou)	a serious, important promise *Sam made a <u>vow</u> to find his missing brother.*

Places

Black Sea	a very salty sea off the coast of Turkey. It has no tide. That is why Othello says it only "flows in one direction."
Egypt	a country in the northeast corner of Africa. It has had a highly developed way of life for over 5,000 years.

The Lost Token

Emilia teased Iago. "I have the handkerchief you so desire!"
Iago seized it eagerly.

Preview: 1. Read the name of the story.
2. Look at the picture.
3. Read the sentences under the picture.
4. Read the first three paragraphs of the story.
5. Then answer the following question.

You learned from your preview that Othello will send away
Desdemona if she is found to
_____ a. be loyal.
_____ b. have great self-control.
_____ c. be guilty.
_____ d. beg often in Cassio's favor.

Turn to the Comprehension Check on page 40 for the right answer.

Now read the story.
Read on to find out what Othello will decide to do.

The Lost Token

"If you learn more, Iago, let me know," said Othello.

"Patience!" Iago suggested. "Let Cassio wait to win back his position. Note how often your wife begs you in his favor. But for now, believe she is loyal to you."

"Be sure I am a man of great self-control," answered Othello. As soon as Iago left, however, his thoughts churned. *If she proves guilty, I'll cut my own heart-strings to send her away!*

At that moment, Desdemona approached. Seeing her, Othello softened. *Her beauty persuades me that she's innocent. She's too lovely to be guilty!*

"Your noble guests are waiting," called Desdemona.

"It's my fault," sighed Othello.

"Your voice is faint. Are you ill?" asked Desdemona.

"My forehead aches."

"Let me tie this around your head. It will take away the pain." She offered him her handkerchief.

"Your handkerchief is too small. Let's go in," said Othello. He pushed away her hand, refusing this small token of love. Neither of them saw the handkerchief flutter to the ground.

When they left, Emilia found it. She recognized it as the one Iago had often asked her to steal. Now, she could embroider the strawberry design on another handkerchief for him, and return this one to Desdemona.

Suddenly, Iago came into the garden. Emilia teased him. "I have the handkerchief you so desire!" Iago seized it eagerly. Suddenly worried, Emilia cried, "Why do you want it? She'll go mad when she finds it missing."

"I need it. And don't tell her what happened to it!" Iago threatened as Emilia left. *I'll plant this in Cassio's lodging,* he thought. *Even a trifle can be strong evidence to a jealous person!* Looking up,

Iago saw Othello coming. The General was muttering to himself.

Coming closer, Othello roared. "You're the one who started this torture! Why did you confuse me?" He grabbed Iago by the throat. "Villain! Make sure you prove she betrayed me!" Iago's reasoning had confused him so much that Othello didn't even think of trying to prove she was innocent. "I desire visible evidence!" he thundered.

Already, jealousy had gnawed deep into Othello's heart. "Do you need to see them actually touch each other?" Othello shook with rage just to imagine the picture Iago was drawing. "Witnessing them together is hard to arrange," said Iago. "Tell me. Have you ever noticed your wife's handkerchief embroidered with strawberries?" asked Iago. "Well, today, I saw Cassio wipe his beard with it."

"That was my first gift to her," stated Othello. Then, he began to swear. "He should have forty thousand lives for me to take! Now I see the truth. All my fond love is gone. Gone!" He knelt and said, in a voice cold as ice, "I vow revenge. Oh blood, blood, blood!"

"Patience!" said Iago. "There is no visible evidence yet. Your mind may change."

"Never, Iago! I am like the Black Sea's icy current. It flows in one direction, and never turns back," Othello answered.

Iago knelt beside Othello. "Oh, stars and all you heavens, witness my vow. I swear to serve the deceived Othello. Let him command. I shall obey."

Othello accepted. "I am most grateful. And I desire your help immediately. In three days, let me hear that Cassio is not alive. I'll find a way to kill her myself," snarled Othello. "I name *you* my lieutenant now."

"I am your own forever," replied Iago.

Meanwhile, Desdemona sent for Cassio. Then, she turned to Emilia. "Have you seen my handkerchief?" she asked. "I'd rather lose a purse full of money than that handkerchief. It's more than a pretty trifle. It was Othello's first gift to me. But, of course, I shouldn't worry. My noble Moor is not a jealous man."

"He isn't?" questioned Emilia. Then, she lied, "No, my lady, I haven't seen it."

Suddenly, Othello arrived. Taking his wife's hand, he said, "This hand is easy for men to love."

"It's the same hand that gave away my heart," she said simply.

Othello let her hand drop. "Joining hands doesn't always mean joining hearts," he said.

Confused, Desdemona tried to distract him. "You promised to speak with Cassio."

The name "Cassio" cut to his heart. Tears rose. "My eyes are watering. Give me your handkerchief, the one embroidered with strawberries," said Othello.

"I don't have it with me," murmured Desdemona.

"A witch from Egypt gave it to my mother, and its magic makes a husband desire only his wife. If a woman loses it, her husband will grow to hate her," said Othello.

Desdemona trembled. "I wish I'd never seen it!" she said nervously.

"Have you lost this token of my love?" he asked fiercely.

"No," she lied, "but what if I had? You are trying to distract me. I ask you to see Cassio."

"Bring the handkerchief!" roared Othello.

"Cassio is loyal to you," continued Desdemona.

"The handkerchief!" roared Othello.

"You are wrong to torture me like this!" Desdemona cried. Othello turned and left.

The Lost Token

COMPREHENSION CHECK

Choose the best answer.

1. Desdemona thought Othello might be ill because
   ___a. his look softened when she approached.
   ___b. he pushed away her hand.
   ___c. his voice was faint.
   ___d. he had great self-control.

2. When Othello's head ached, he
   ___a. blamed Iago.
   ___b. asked Desdemona for her handkerchief.
   ___c. refused to see his noble guests.
   ___d. refused Desdemona's offer to help him.

3. After Iago got the embroidered handkerchief, he planned to
   ___a. show it to Othello.
   ___b. hide it in Cassio's lodgings.
   ___c. return it to Desdemona.
   ___d. return it to Emilia.

4. Othello's anger is stirred when
   ___a. Iago witnesses Desdemona and Cassio together.
   ___b. he tells Iago that the Black Sea "never turns back."
   ___c. Iago calls him "the deceived Othello."
   ___d. Iago tells Othello that he saw Cassio with the embroidered handkerchief.

5. Iago says, "Even a trifle can be strong evidence to a jealous person." In that statement, the "trifle" means
   ___a. Emilia's teasing.
   ___b. the General's muttering to himself.
   ___c. Othello's aching forehead.
   ___d. the handkerchief embroidered with strawberries.

6. Which sentence is *not* a reason why the embroidered handkerchief is important?
   ___a. Othello believed it was magic.
   ___b. It was Othello's first gift to Desdemona.
   ___c. It had a strawberry design on it.
   ___d. It had belonged to Othello's mother.

7. Othello gives Iago three days to
   ___a. kill Cassio.
   ___b. become Othello's lieutenant.
   ___c. make Emilia tell the truth.
   ___d. distract Desdemona.

8. When Othello asked Desdemona for her embroidered handkerchief, she
   ___a. told Othello she had lost it.
   ___b. thanked Othello for giving it to her.
   ___c. complained his mother was a witch.
   ___d. became nervous and wished she'd never seen it.

9. Another name for this story could be
   ___a. "Too Lovely to Be Guilty."
   ___b. "Imagine Iago's Drawing."
   ___c. "Jealousy Gnaws Deeper."
   ___d. "Emilia's Lies."

10. This story is mainly about
    ___a. Othello's patience.
    ___b. Othello's loss of self-control.
    ___c. Cassio's being loyal to Othello.
    ___d. Desdemona's support of Cassio.

Check your answers with the key on page 67.

The Lost Token

VOCABULARY CHECK

confuse	desire	embroider	innocent	loyal	visible

I. Sentences to Finish
Fill in the blank in each sentence with the correct key word from the box above.

1. It is easy to _____ the twins because they look and dress alike.

2. The three brothers are very _____ to each other in times of trouble.

3. Gemma finally picked the pattern she would _____ on her sweater.

4. Amy kept her deepest _____ a secret.

5. The road was hardly _____ in the thick fog.

6. When the judge pronounced her _____, June breathed a sigh of relief.

II. Mixed-up Words
Unscramble the letters in Column A to spell out the key words. Then draw a line from each word to its meaning in Column B.

Column A	Column B
1. neonitnc _____	a. to sew designs onto cloth
2. esunofc _____	b. to wish or long for earnestly
3. ylloa _____	c. able to be seen
4. irreebmod _____	d. true and faithful
5. bvsiiel _____	e. not guilty; doing no wrong
6. resedi _____	f. to mix up; to disturb one's thinking so that nothing is certain

Check your answers with the key on page 70.

This page may be reproduced for classroom use.

A Heart of Stone

PREPARATION

Key Words

civilized (siv´ə līzd) 1. well-developed in art, science, and way of life
The people of China were highly <u>civilized</u> in ancient times.
2. showing good manners
"Act <u>civilized</u>!" growled Ted, when his younger brother grabbed all the candy at once.

memory (mem´ər ē) 1. the power to remember
The accident caused Sheila to lose her <u>memory</u>.
2. a person, thing, or event that is remembered
The <u>memory</u> of Lora's smile was fresh in Jeff's mind.

observe (əb zėrv´) 1. to see and note; to notice
Did you <u>observe</u> the new traffic sign at the corner?
2. to examine for some special purpose; to study
The scientist stayed up at night to <u>observe</u> radio waves from the stars.

plead (plēd) 1. to ask for earnestly
Juan waited for his brother to <u>plead</u> for forgiveness before he offered to shake his hand.
2. to argue, giving reasons
Marina was ready to <u>plead</u> with her parents for use of the family car.

sin (sin) 1. to break the law of God on purpose
Does a person <u>sin</u> if he or she does something wrong without knowing it's wrong?
2. a wrong, done on purpose
Angelo admitted his <u>sin</u> of jealousy, and asked God's help to change his way of acting.

stun (stun) to surprise, making one confused and not able to reason
Edna knew that the news of her arrest would <u>stun</u> her family.

A Heart of Stone

Necessary Words

gestures (jes´ chərz) moving parts of one's body to help express ideas or feelings
Seeing our gestures, the saleswoman came to help us.

murder (mėr´ dər) to kill a person without permission of the law
The thief had not planned to murder anyone at the bank.

strangle (strang´gl) to kill by cutting off one's air supply
The farmer used his bare hands to strangle the chicken.

tempt (tempt) to try to make someone do something
"I don't have enough money," said Debra. "So. don't tempt me to buy a new car like yours."

People

Bianca a woman who has fallen madly in love with Cassio. He treats her like a girlfriend.

A Heart of Stone

"This is a token from another lover!" accused Bianca.

Preview: 1. Read the name of the story.
2. Look at the picture.
3. Read the sentence under the picture.
4. Read the first six paragraphs of the story.
5. Then answer the following question.

You learned from your preview that
_____ a. Emilia is jealous.
_____ b. Iago is angry.
_____ c. Cassio is not himself.
_____ d. Othello usually controlled his passions.

Turn to the Comprehension Check on page 46 for the right answer.

Now read the story.
Read on to find out if Othello still believes Iago.

A Heart of Stone

Desdemona was worried. "The handkerchief must be magic!" she said.

"Don't let anything a man does stun you," said Emilia.

Iago and Cassio came to plead for Desdemona's help again. "My Lord is not himself now," she sighed. "Every time I speak, he gets angry."

"Angry?" echoed Iago. "Something must be very wrong! I've seen him control his passions when a cannon blew up all his soldiers. And even when his brother was killed right next to him!"

"Ruling Cyprus may be difficult," said Desdemona after Iago left. "I'll try to be more patient."

"Is he jealous?" asked Emilia.

"I never gave him reason to be," replied Desdemona.

"Jealous people don't need reasons," explained Emilia. "That's just the way they are."

After the women left Cassio alone, a familiar voice called to him. He smiled. Bianca hurried over.

"I was just coming to see you," lied Cassio to his girlfriend. He handed her a handkerchief. "Will you embroider this design for me? I found it in my room, and I want it copied before the owner asks for it."

While Cassio and Bianca spoke, two other men were imagining how Cassio had been with Desdemona.

"Maybe they kiss in private," suggested Iago.

"That's wrong!" cried Othello.

"But maybe their hearts remain innocent," Iago added.

"They tempt the devil!" exclaimed Othello. "It isn't possible to act like that and be innocent!"

"If I gave my wife a handkerchief, it would belong to her," said Iago. "She could give it to any man she pleases."

"Could she give away her honor, too?" asked Othello.

"You can't see honor," said Iago, "but you can see a handkerchief."

"The memory returns like a bird circling over the bodies of the dying," Othello said in a tortured voice. "You saw Cassio with my handkerchief, didn't you!" It was as if he were hearing the news for the first time.

"What if I had been able to observe them together?" asked Iago. "What if I heard him boasting...?"

"Has he said anything? What did he say?" insisted Othello.

Iago answered, pausing for greater effect, "He said-- that he did -- I don't know what."

"What?!!" shouted Othello, and his body began to quiver. "Jealousy wouldn't cast such a shadow over me unless this were true. Words alone could never make me tremble like this!" And he fell down in a faint.

"My poison is working!" Iago murmured.

Just then, Cassio came by. "What's wrong?" he asked.

"It's his second fit in two days. He must stay quiet. Step away until it passes," said Iago. "Later, come speak with me alone."

After Othello had come to, Iago asked, "Did you hurt your head?"

"Are you laughing at me?" demanded Othello. To himself, he wondered, *Is Iago teasing me about my new reputation?* He knew that cuckolds were often pictured with horns growing out of their foreheads.

"Act like a man!" Iago scolded.

"A horned man is a monster and a beast!" answered Othello.

"The civilized world has many. A million men are betrayed every day," said Iago.

"Iago, you are certainly wise," confessed Othello.

"Now, hurry and hide!" said Iago. "I want you to observe me with Cassio." He pointed to a spot where Othello would be able to see them. But he would be too far to hear them clearly. Then, Iago explained. "Cassio came. He was stunned to see you fallen. I made up a good excuse. When he returns, I'll encourage him to talk about Desdemona. Observe very closely Cassio's face and gestures. Listen well, but hold your patience!" Iago's evil mind was already planning how he would get the desired effect from this meeting.

"I will be most patient -- and most bloody!" insisted Othello.

"All in good time," said Iago. "Now, hide!"

Ha! thought Iago, *I'll talk to Cassio about Bianca to make him laugh. Cassio's excited gestures while he's talking will drive Othello crazy. In his jealousy, he'll feel certain that Cassio is laughing about being with Desdemona.*

Just then, Cassio arrived. "How are you, Lieutenant?" said Iago.

"Worse!" answered Cassio.

Loudly enough for Othello to hear, Iago said, "You'll be sure to get what you want if you beg Desdemona." Then, almost in a whisper, he added, "Now, if you'd asked Bianca for help, she'd have won your position back instantly!" Cassio laughed loudly. "Are you tempted to marry her?" asked Iago, loudly.

As the laughter continued, Othello grew angrier. He imagined the lovers together. *You monster, Cassio!* he thought.

Just then, Bianca came by. She threw a handkerchief at Cassio. "I can't believe your foolish excuse! Copy the design! I won't! It's a token from another lover," accused Bianca. She turned and walked out. Cassio followed, pleading with her.

Othello came out from hiding, saying, "How shall I murder him?"

"Did you hear him laugh at his sin? And did you see your handkerchief?" replied Iago.

The reminder stunned the Moor. "Was that mine?" he asked.

"Yours!" answered Iago.

"My sweet wife betrayed me," groaned Othello. "No, she shall not live, for my heart is turned to stone! Yet, she's so gifted and gentle that she could make a bear civilized," he added, softening. "Oh, the pity of it!"

"If you feel that way, let her live and continue sinning," said Iago.

"I'll chop her to pieces!" shouted Othello. "Make me a cuckold?" And he dismissed the memory of his wife's gentle character. "Get some poison."

"You should strangle her instead, in the same bed where she betrayed you," suggested Iago, "and I'll murder Cassio by midnight."

"Good, very good! I'll strangle her," repeated Othello.

A Heart of Stone

COMPREHENSION CHECK

Choose the best answer.

1. In battle, Iago saw Othello
   ___a. blow up all his soldiers.
   ___b. get angry.
   ___c. kill his brother.
   ___d. control his passions.

2. Desdemona says she never gave Othello reason to be
   ___a. jealous.
   ___b. angry.
   ___c. patient.
   ___d. innocent.

3. Which character in this story really understands jealous people?
   ___a. Bianca
   ___b. Emilia
   ___c. Desdemona
   ___d. Cassio

4. Othello says, "The memory returns like a bird circling over the bodies of the dying." He means that he remembers
   ___a. how his brother died.
   ___b. the war in Cyprus.
   ___c. how the Turkish fleet sank.
   ___d. that Iago saw Cassio with Desdemona's embroidered handkerchief.

5. Othello falls down in a faint
   ___a. after Iago poisons him.
   ___b. after Cassio comes by.
   ___c. after Iago tells him about Cassio's boasting.
   ___d. after Desdemona kisses Cassio.

6. Iago scolds Othello to "act like a man," because Othello had
   ___a. fainted.
   ___b. hurt his head.
   ___c. laughed at Iago.
   ___d. not acted civilized.

7. Iago wants Othello to hide so Othello can
   ___a. trap Cassio and murder him.
   ___b. listen to Desdemona.
   ___c. hear all Cassio's words.
   ___d. watch Cassio, but not hear him clearly.

8. Cassio used excited gestures while speaking with Iago because Iago
   ___a. made Cassio angry.
   ___b. tempted Cassio to fight.
   ___c. laughed at Cassio.
   ___d. joked about Bianca and made Cassio laugh a lot.

9. Another name for this story could be
   ___a. "Pleading for Help."
   ___b. "Wise Iago."
   ___c. "Jealousy's Shadow."
   ___d. "The Monster, Cassio."

10. This story is mainly about
    ___a. Cassio's girlfriends.
    ___b. jealousy's effect on Othello.
    ___c. Iago's plan to murder Cassio.
    ___d. Desdemona's worries about Othello.

Check your answers with the key on page 67.

This page may be reproduced for classroom use.

A Heart of Stone

VOCABULARY CHECK

civilized	memory	observe	plead	sin	stun

I. Sentences to Finish
Fill in the blank in each sentence with the correct key word from the box above.

1. By God's command, stealing what does not belong to you is a _____.

2. Trish's _____ of her family's vacation in Maine was a happy one.

3. Yaffa decided to ask for higher pay, but she refused to _____ for it.

4. Joel would _____ his coach by placing first in the race.

5. If you wish to become a teacher, you will have the opportunity to _____ other teachers and practice teaching their classes during your training.

6. Courtesy and good manners are signs of a _____ people.

II. Matching
Write the letter of the correct meaning from Column B next to the key word in Column A.

Column A	Column B
_____1. plead	a. surprise, making one confused
_____2. civilized	b. well-developed in way of life; showing good manners
_____3. stun	c. the act of remembering
_____4. observe	d. to argue, giving reasons; to ask for earnestly
_____5. sin	e. to notice; to study for some special purpose
_____6. memory	f. a wrong, done on purpose

Check your answers with the key on page 71.

Whose Scheme Will Work?

PREPARATION

Key Words

behavior   (bi hā´vyər)   a way of acting
Ginny is embarrassed by her son's rude <u>behavior</u>.

convince   (kən vins´)   to make someone feel sure; to cause to believe;
to persuade with proof
Connor tried to <u>convince</u> his brother to support someone else for president.

fury   (fyùr´ē)   1. wild, fierce anger; rage
When they came too close to the cubs, the mother bear attacked in a sudden <u>fury</u>.
2. fierceness
The storm's <u>fury</u> sank every galley in the fleet.

obedient   (ō bē´dē ənt)   doing what one is told; willing to obey
Emma thought her dog was <u>obedient</u> until he broke his collar and chased after a cat.

relative   (rel´ə tiv)   a person who belongs to the same family as another
Laura was a distant <u>relative</u>, but she had the same green eyes as the rest of the family.

scheme   (skēm)   a plan, especially an evil one
Jessie's <u>scheme</u> to blame her brother for the robbery failed, because a neighbor witnessed her leaving the house.

Whose Scheme Will Work?

Necessary Words

curse (kėrs) 1. to use rude language
Alex began to <u>curse</u> when the truck moved in front of his car.
2. to ask for evil to happen to someone or something
In the story about Macbeth, the queen of the witches put an evil <u>curse</u> on him.

false (fôls) 1. used to deceive; deceiving
Bridget gave a <u>false</u> excuse, so she wouldn't have to tell her parents where she had been.
2. not faithful; not loyal
A <u>false</u> friend will not keep a secret.

misunderstand (mis'un'dər stand') 1. to understand wrongly
If you <u>misunderstand</u> the directions for your new sewing machine, ask for help.
2. to take in a wrong sense
A nervous or fearful person may <u>misunderstand</u> your friendly gesture.

promotion (prə mō'shən) a move to a more important position
Brandon did all the work, but Mark received the <u>promotion.</u>

People

Lodovico Desdemona's relative and a noble messenger for the Duke

Things

crocodile tears pretended tears or sadness

Whose Scheme Will Work?

*Othello receives a letter from the Duke asking him
to return to Venice.*

Preview: 1. Read the name of the story.
2. Look at the picture.
3. Read the sentence under the picture.
4. Read the first three paragraphs of the story.
5. Then answer the following question.

You learned from your preview that Desdemona
_____ a. is Iago's relative.
_____ b. received a letter from the Duke.
_____ c. will soon fix Cassio's friendship with Othello.
_____ d. is Lodovico's relative.

Turn to the Comprehension Check on page 52 for the right answer.

Now read the story.
Read on to find out if Lodovico discovers Iago's evil scheme.

Whose Scheme Will Work?

The sound of a loud trumpet stunned Othello. "It must be men from Venice," said Iago. Lodovico, a relative of Desdemona, came in. He gave Othello a letter from the Duke. While the Moor read it, Lodovico spoke with Iago. "How is Cassio?" he asked.

"Living," said Iago.

Desdemona tried to explain. "Cassio's friendship with my husband is broken." Then, she turned to Othello, and said, "But you will soon fix it."

"Don't be so sure your scheme will work!" muttered Othello.

"What do you mean?" she asked.

Othello pretended to be reading his letter. Lodovico spoke up. "You were saying that the two friends have separated?"

"I value Cassio greatly and would do anything to bring them together," answered Desdemona.

Othello began to curse. "The letter may be upsetting him," explained Lodovico. "The Duke is asking him to return to Venice. Cassio will be governor of Cyprus."

"I'm glad of it!" said Desdemona, hoping the change might end Othello's strange behavior.

Othello managed to misunderstand her. He thought Desdemona was glad for her lover's promotion. In fury, he struck her.

"I could never convince a soul that I've witnessed this," Lodovico said sternly. "You've made her cry!"

"Crocodile tears," said Othello. "Your tears are false, devil! Get out of my sight!" he ordered angrily.

Desdemona left quietly. "See how obedient she is!" said Lodovico. "Call her back!"

"Mistress!" Othello called, in an insulting voice. When she turned around, Othello told Lodovico, "See how she turned. She turned on me! As you say, she is obedient. Look at her weep! She pretends." Then, he shouted at her roughly, "Get out of here!" He turned to Lodovico again. "I'll go to Venice as the Duke ordered. You can keep Cyprus!"

Othello's behavior stunned Lodovico. "Is this the man respected by all of Venice?" he asked after the Moor had left. "Has he lost his wits?"

"If he were crazy," said Iago, "at least that would be an excuse."

"There's no excuse to strike his wife!" answered Lodovico.

"I doubt that'll be the worst he'll do to your relative," hinted Iago.

Meanwhile, Othello found Emilia, and began to question her about Cassio and Desdemona.

"I'm always with them. They never whisper or send me away," insisted Emilia.

She's loyal to my wife, thought Othello as Emilia left to get Desdemona. *She'll never betray her.*

"Look at my face!" ordered Othello when Desdemona came. "Let me see your eyes." He gestured for Emilia to leave.

"I hear the fury in your voice, but I don't understand your words," cried Desdemona in distress.

"You are as false as hell!" screamed Othello, cursing.

"How am I false, my lord?" she pleaded, as he pushed her away. "You misunderstand me. Perhaps you are upset because of the letter? Do you think my father has had you called back? Oh, please, don't blame me for it! If you have lost his friendship, remember that I have lost him, too!"

"If heaven tortured me with any other problem, I could bear it," said Othello with passion. "But not here, in my heart! There all my hopes and feelings are found. Life pours from my heart like a spring of water. Let that spring dry up, I have no life! And if the spring be not pure anymore, I have no hope! Here, Desdemona, where you were in my heart, the spring is evil as hell!"

"Does my lord not think me honest?" Desdemona questioned.

"Yes," answered Othello, "you're sweet and lovely -- like a weed! My whole body aches with desire for you. But I wish you were never born! You betrayed our marriage! Don't pretend to be innocent!"

"I never sinned," she said. "No other man has ever touched me."

"Excuse me," said Othello. "I confused you with my evil wife!" And he stormed out of the room.

"What's wrong with your husband?" asked Emilia as she came in.

"I have none," sighed Desdemona, close to a faint. "I don't know. Please, Emilia, call your husband."

"He said she sinned with other men!" said Emilia to Iago when he arrived. "She gave up everything for him, and he insults her! No doubt some villain who's trying to win a promotion convinced Othello with lies. Heaven should put a whip in every honest hand and chase that villain through the world!"

"Speak more softly," Iago urged.

"Why should I?" growled Emilia. "Some fool like that put suspicion in your head about me and the Moor. Remember?"

"Iago, good friend, help me!" pleaded Desdemona.

"Othello's worried about business. Don't be upset," said Iago. "Listen, the trumpets announce a feast for the visitors. Go in, and don't weep. Everything will be fine."

A few minutes later, Roderigo came to Iago in a fury. Suddenly, he was very critical. "You gave my jewels to Desdemona. You said she received them and desired me," he said. "But nothing in her behavior convinces me that her feelings have changed. Your scheme has failed! I will ask her to return my jewels. If she won't, you'll be responsible for paying me back!"

Iago had to think quickly. If Roderigo spoke with Desdemona, his scheme would be ruined. "Tonight, you'll prove your courage," Iago said firmly. Then, he told Roderigo about Cassio's promotion. "If Cassio becomes governor, the Moor will take Desdemona to his home far from Venice. Do you dare to help me get rid of Cassio?" he tempted.

"I'll need more reasons than that to convince me," said Roderigo.

"You'll be convinced," answered Iago.

51

Whose Scheme Will Work?

COMPREHENSION CHECK

Choose the best answer.

1. Desdemona tried to explain Othello's broken friendship with Cassio to
   ___a. all of Venice.
   ___b. Lodovico.
   ___c. the Moor.
   ___d. Emilia.

2. Which sentence is *not* true of the Duke's letter to Othello?
   ___a. Othello must return to Venice.
   ___b. Lodovico will become governor.
   ___c. Othello may feel upset by the letter.
   ___d. Cassio will get a promotion.

3. When did Othello strike Desdemona in fury?
   ___a. when he failed to understand Desdemona's words, "I'm glad of it!"
   ___b. after Lodovico said, "You've made her cry!"
   ___c. before the Duke sent Lodovico to Cyprus.
   ___d. when Desdemona said, "I value Cassio greatly..."

4. Iago hints that Othello may do worse than strike Desdemona, because Iago knows
   ___a. the Moor is crazy.
   ___b. all of Venice respects Othello.
   ___c. Othello plans to strangle his wife.
   ___d. Othello plans to poison his wife.

5. Who thinks that Emilia will never betray Desdemona?
   ___a. Iago
   ___b. Desdemona, herself
   ___c. Cassio
   ___d. Othello

6. Desdemona wonders if Othello is upset because her father
   ___a. misunderstands Othello.
   ___b. may have asked the Duke to order Othello back to Venice.
   ___c. shed crocodile tears.
   ___d. sent Lodovico to Cyprus.

7. The one problem that Othello feels he cannot bear is
   ___a. Desdemona misunderstanding him.
   ___b. seeing Cassio become governor.
   ___c. returning to Venice.
   ___d. Desdemona betraying his love.

8. Who thinks that someone desiring a promotion has lied to Othello about his wife?
   ___a. Iago
   ___b. Emilia
   ___c. Roderigo
   ___d. Lodovico

9. Another name for this story could be
   ___a. "Othello is Distracted."
   ___b. "Roderigo's Scheme."
   ___c. "Desdemona's Crocodile Tears."
   ___d. "Othello's Fury Grows."

10. This story is mainly about
    ___a. Desdemona pleading for Cassio.
    ___b. Iago convincing Roderigo that their scheme will succeed.
    ___c. Othello cursing the Duke.
    ___d. Othello showing how convinced he is that Desdemona has betrayed him.

Check your answers with the key on page 67.

This page may be reproduced for classroom use.

Whose Scheme Will Work?

VOCABULARY CHECK

behavior	convince	fury	obedient	relative	scheme

I. Sentences to Finish
Fill in the blank in each sentence with the correct key word from the box above.

1. Which _____ can't join you for Thanksgiving dinner?

2. "Has Eden's _____ improved?" the judge asked the prison guard.

3. The wind whipped through the trees with great _____ during the storm.

4. Roberta's _____ to raise money by washing cars succeeded very well.

5. The governor was able to _____ the citizens of his honesty after he was falsely accused of stealing.

6. A guide dog for a blind person must be a very _____ animal.

II. Word Use
Put a check next to YES if the sentence makes sense. Put a check next to NO if the sentence does not make sense.

1. Jackie smiled with a **fury**. _____Yes _____No

2. The clown's **behavior** caused everyone to laugh. _____Yes _____No

3. **Obedient** children do what their parents ask. _____Yes _____No

4. Every **relative** in Delia's family came to her birthday party. _____Yes _____No

5. If you pretend to be a **scheme**, you won't have friends. _____Yes _____No

6. "Don't **convince** me for your problems!" said Anne. "They're not my fault." _____Yes _____No

Check your answers with the key on page 71.

This page may be reproduced for classroom use.

Murder in the Dark

PREPARATION

Key Words

instruct   (in strukt´)

to teach, to train; to direct how to do
Aunt Ethel likes to instruct the servants on how to wash her expensive china.

resolution   (rez´ə lu´shən)

1. making up your mind to do or not do something
Jen made a New Year's resolution to exercise every day.
2. power of holding firmly to a purpose
The sale sign weakened Jorge's resolution to stop buying tools.

risk   (risk)

to invite possible harm
Gina decided to risk driving on the icy road.

scorn   (skôrn)

1. to look down upon; despise
Honest people scorn those who tell lies.
2. reject or refuse as low or wrong; rejection
Fred found his boss's scorn for the farmworkers hard to accept.

thrust   (thrust)

1. to stab
The actor practiced how to thrust his sword without harming his stage enemy.
2. to push with force
Even the tiniest flower must thrust its roots into the ground to live.

weapon   (wep´ ən)

any object or tool used to hurt, wound or kill
The frightened young man put down his weapon when he saw that the stray animal was friendly.

Murder in the Dark

Necessary Words

shroud   (shroud)   a cloth used to wrap a dead person's body
before it is buried
> *The soldier who died in the battle was so tall that the
> villagers did not have a cloth long enough for his
> <u>shroud</u>.*

People

Gratiano   Desdemona's uncle who traveled to Cyprus with Lodovico

Murder in the Dark

As she walked Desdemona to her room,
Emilia spoke her thoughts aloud.

Preview: 1. Read the name of the story.
2. Look at the picture.
3. Read the sentence under the picture.
4. Read the first four paragraphs of the story.
5. Then answer the following question.

You learned from your preview that Desdemona
_____ a. wants to dismiss Emilia.
_____ b. wants to walk with Lodovico.
_____ c. still loves Cassio.
_____ d. still loves Othello.

Turn to the Comprehension Check on page 58 for the right answer.

Now read the story.
Read on to find out who will be murdered.

Murder in the Dark

"Good night, Madam," said Lodovico when the feast was over.

"Won't you come for a short walk with me before you leave?" Othello asked Lodovico. Then, Othello turned to his wife. In a soft voice he said, "Leave now. Go to bed quickly. I'll come to you very soon. Oh, and dismiss Emilia for the night."

As she walked Desdemona to her room, Emilia spoke her thoughts aloud. "Othello seems gentler than he did earlier." But, when she heard that Othello had ordered her to leave her mistress so quickly, Emilia became anxious. "I wish you'd never seen him!"

"Even when he's rough and angry, my heart finds beauty in him," Desdemona replied. Then, Emilia helped her get ready for bed.

That afternoon Desdemona had asked Emilia to make the bed with the sheets from their marriage night. She had hoped they would remind Othello of the promise of a long, happy life together. But now, when Emilia told her she had made the bed, Desdemona said, "It doesn't matter. I was being foolish. If I die before you, make my shroud with those sheets."

"Don't talk of shrouds!" Emilia warned her. Emilia pretended to scorn such thoughts of death, but she was worried. As Emilia finished helping her, Desdemona began to sing a sad love song:

I'll wear a circle of willow
around my head.
Let nobody blame him,
I accept his scorn...
"Oh, that's not the next line!" Desdemona added, becoming confused. "Listen...who's knocking at the door?"

"It's the wind," said Emilia.

"No woman would deceive her husband in the way my husband accuses me," said Desdemona. "You wouldn't deceive your husband for all the world, would you, Emilia?"

"The world would be a great prize for such a small sin. I'd risk being punished and turning my husband into a cuckold if it would make him a king," said Emilia. "Besides, when women betray their husbands, it's the husbands' faults. They go off with other women, or guard us with jealousy. Sometimes, they strike us. We can accept their behavior, but we can also have some revenge. Husbands should learn that we have the same desires and weaknesses they have. Their sins instruct us how to sin, too."

"Their bad behavior won't become an excuse for me, but it will teach me what to avoid," said Desdemona.

Down a dark street, Iago instructs Roderigo on how to kill Cassio. "Hide behind this wall. Keep your weapon ready. And when he comes, thrust your sword home. This deed will win everything, or ruin us completely. Don't let your resolution fail you!"

Iago stepped away. But he stayed near just in case something would go wrong. If either man were killed, Iago would win. He hated them both. Roderigo wanted Iago to return the jewels he had supposedly given to Desdemona. Instead, Iago had spent them. As for Cassio, his good life and fortune made Iago jealous. And what if Cassio learned of the rumors Iago had spread to destroy his reputation?

Footsteps echoed down the street. Recognizing them as Cassio's, Roderigo jumped from behind the wall. He stabbed Cassio, but Cassio's thick coat protected him from the weapon. Cassio thrust his sword into Roderigo. Iago attacked from behind, but only wounded Cassio's leg. Then, he slipped back into the darkness, leaving the two men screaming for help.

Othello recognized Cassio's voice. *Cassio is dead! Iago kept his promise!* he thought. *His deed instructs me. Now I am moved to do the same to Desdemona.*

As Othello set out, two of Desdemona's relatives were on their way to tell Cassio of his promotion. Fear filled Lodovico and Gratiano, as they heard screams.

"Murder, murder! Oh, help!" yelled Cassio.

Cyprus was not as civilized as Venice. The two men wouldn't risk getting any closer, in case it was a trap set by robbers.

"Won't anybody help?" cried Roderigo. "I bleed to death!"

"Someone is coming with a light and weapons," said Gratiano. Acting as if he'd just heard the screams, Iago came running.

When Roderigo called for help again, Cassio warned the men that he was one of the attackers. Iago hurriedly stabbed Roderigo. "Iago, you cruel dog!" gasped Roderigo as he died.

Next, Iago took off his own shirt. He bound up Cassio's wound. Then, Bianca appeared out of the darkness. Iago looked at her with scorn. He hinted that she was responsible for the attack. Then, Iago held a light over the man he'd murdered moments before. He pretended to be surprised. The others heard him gasp. "It's my friend Roderigo!"

Cassio didn't recognize Roderigo from the night he had gotten drunk. "I don't know him at all."

Bianca was crying over Cassio. As he was carried off to the doctor, Iago used her behavior as evidence against her. "Look at how pale she is. See the fear in her eyes. She must have planned Cassio's murder!" So, he arrested her.

When Emilia arrived at the scene of distress, Iago sent her to tell Othello about the attack. As she started back toward her mistress's room, the Moor was already kneeling by his sleeping wife.

She must die, or she'll betray more men, he thought as he kissed her. Her sweet breath on his cheek threatened his resolution to kill her. *It's enough to make Justice break her sword! But I will kill you and love you after. I must weep, but mine are cruel tears!* As he leaned over to kiss her one last time, his tears spilled onto her face. She began to awaken.

57

Murder in the Dark

COMPREHENSION CHECK

Choose the best answer.

1. Othello does not want Desdemona to
   ___a. say good night to Lodovico.
   ___b. keep Emilia on duty for the night.
   ___c. leave with Emilia.
   ___d. go to bed right away.

2. Why does Desdemona say, "I was being foolish"?
   ___a. Because she thought Lodovico could change Othello's mind about Cassio
   ___b. Because she dismissed Emilia
   ___c. Because using the sheets from their marriage night won't solve her problem with Othello
   ___d. Because she finds beauty in Othello "even when he's rough and angry"

3. Desdemona sings a sad love song
   ___a. while Emilia makes the bed.
   ___b. after Emilia talks about husbands and wives betraying each other.
   ___c. when Othello kisses her for the last time.
   ___d. after talking about dying.

4. What does Emilia want husbands to learn about women?
   ___a. that they should be guarded with jealousy.
   ___b. that they will never take revenge.
   ___c. that they should not excuse bad behavior.
   ___d. that they have the same weaknesses and desires as men.

5. How does Desdemona look upon men's weaknesses and bad behavior?
   ___a. They will teach her how to sin, too.
   ___b. They will teach her what to avoid.
   ___c. She wants revenge.
   ___d. She wants to die.

6. While Roderigo waits in the dark to kill Cassio, Iago stays near because
   ___a. he doesn't trust Roderigo.
   ___b. he wants to kill Cassio himself.
   ___c. he hears footsteps and needs to hide.
   ___d. he wants to be sure that the evil scheme succeeds.

7. Who dies in the street attack?
   ___a. Roderigo
   ___b. Lodovico
   ___c. Cassio
   ___d. Gratiano

8. Who is blamed for the attack on Cassio?
   ___a. Iago
   ___b. Roderigo
   ___c. the Moor
   ___d. Bianca

9. Another name for this story could be
   ___a. "Betrayals."
   ___b. "A Good Resolution."
   ___c. "Husbands' Faults."
   ___d. "One Last Kiss."

10. This story is mainly about
   ___a. Emilia feeling anxious.
   ___b. Roderigo failing to kill Cassio.
   ___c. Iago's mistake in killing Roderigo.
   ___d. Othello growing stronger in his resolution to kill Desdemona.

Check your answers with the key on page 67.

This page may be reproduced for classroom use.

Murder in the Dark

VOCABULARY CHECK

instruct	resolution	risk	scorn	thrust	weapon

I. Sentences to Finish
Fill in the blank in each sentence with the correct key word from the box above.

1. To express _____ for any person is rude behavior.

2. "Would you _____ your life to save another person?" Sheila asked Jasmine.

3. "Drop your _____ !" ordered the police officer.

4. Mother birds _____ their young to fly.

5. Angel _____ his tiny fist into the jar, hoping to get some candy.

6. Elena's _____ to finish high school weakened when she heard about the new exams.

II. Circle the letter in front of the best answer.

1. Reno was so skilled in judo that he didn't need a _____ to defend himself.
   a. scorn   b. risk   c. instruct   d. weapon

2. The artist will _____ each pupil in how to draw the design.
   a. risk   b. instruct   c. scorn   d. thrust

3. Everyone could see the look of _____ on Cher's face.
   a. scorn   b. weapon   c. thrust   d. risk

4. Lisa followed her dreams with strong _____.
   a. instruct   b. scorn   c. resolution   d. weapon

5. "Don't _____ ruining your health by smoking!" Jen begged her boyfriend.
   a. risk   b. thrust   c. resolution   d. instruct

6. The warrior _____ his sword into the earth as a sign of surrender.
   a. weapon   b. risk   c. instruct   d. thrust

Check your answers with the key on page 71.

59

A Guilty Death

PREPARATION

Key Words

crime (krīm)

1. an evil or wrong act
   It is a crime not to help the poor if you are able to.
2. an act that is against the law
   The police found fingerprints at the scene of the robbery, but they never knew who was responsible for the crime.

failure (fāl´yər)

1. someone or something that has not succeeded
   Carl felt like a failure when he didn't win any medals in the race.
2. a plan that ends without success
   Their experiment to make diamonds out of coal was a failure.

mercy (mėr´sē)

a kinder way of acting than justice demands
Are you familiar with the story where the mouse begs the lion to show mercy?

sacrifice (sak´rə fīs)

an act of offering to a god
Ancient peoples often chose animals to sacrifice to their gods.

smother (smuŦH´ər)

to make unable to get air; to kill by keeping air from
Don't let the baby play with that thick blanket; it might smother her.

sob (sob)

to cry or sigh with short, quick breaths
Elio began to sob when he heard the sad news.

A Guilty Death

Necessary Words

commit   (kə mit´)   to do something, usually something wrong
Lisa was deeply distressed to learn that her sister had tried to <u>commit</u> suicide.

fatal   (fā´tl)   1. causing death
My friend Carol died in that <u>fatal</u> airplane crash.
2. causing ruin
The captain made a <u>fatal</u> mistake when he turned the wrong switch and the ship's engine was destroyed.

suicide   (sü´ə sīd)   the act of killing oneself on purpose
Some people believe that smoking is a form of <u>suicide</u>.

A Guilty Death

"Have mercy on me, Othello!" cried Desdemona.

Preview: 1. Read the name of the story.
2. Look at the picture.
3. Read the sentence under the picture.
4. Read the first seven paragraphs of the story.
5. Then answer the following question.

You learned from your preview that Othello intends to

_____ a. pray for forgiveness.

_____ b. kill his wife.

_____ c. show mercy to Desdemona.

_____ d. accuse Cassio.

Turn to the Comprehension Check on page 64 for the right answer.

Now read the story.

Read on to find out who will die a guilty death.

A Guilty Death

"Othello?" Desdemona whispered, slowly opening her eyes.

"Do you need forgiveness for any crime?" Othello asked. "Pray for it. I don't want to send you to hell; I don't wish to kill your soul."

"Heaven have mercy," cried Desdemona; "I haven't done anything wrong! Why do you speak of killing?"

"You gave my handkerchief to Cassio," accused Othello.

"No, by my life and soul," she said. "Send for Cassio. Ask him."

"Don't tell lies on your deathbed," he warned.

"Have mercy on me, Othello!"

But he would not listen as Desdemona vowed that Cassio was only a friend. "I never gave him that token of your love," she insisted.

"I saw it in his hand!" shouted Othello. In his mind, her death was to be a sacrifice for her sins. But the more she claimed to be innocent, the more his jealousy raged. It caused him to worry. *If I kill her in anger, I will be murdering her, not making a sacrifice,* he thought.

"Cassio can't help. Iago has taken care of that!" snarled Othello.

"What? Is he dead? He is betrayed!" she exclaimed in deep distress. "Oh, Lord!" Desdemona began to sob. She pleaded for time. "Let me say one last prayer!"

"It's too late," muttered Othello. And he began to smother her.

"My lord, my lord!" cried Emilia as she pounded on the door. Desdemona was fighting for air. Othello wondered, *Should I have given her a gentler death?* Finally, she stopped moving.

Emilia was still pounding on the door. *She will want to speak to my wife,* thought Othello. As he looked down at the limp body he had just smothered, he reminded himself, *I have no wife.* To hide his crime, he pulled the curtains around the bed. Then, he unlocked the door.

Emilia rushed into the room. "Cassio has killed Roderigo!"

"Roderigo?" repeated Othello, puzzled. "And was Cassio killed?"

Emilia replied, "No, only hurt."

Just at that moment, Emilia heard a faint voice. "Lord, what cry is that?" she exclaimed.

"That? What?" said Othello.

Emilia pulled aside the bed curtains. "Sweet Desdemona!" she shrieked. Who did this to you?"

"Nobody. I myself." With these words, Desdemona died. She would let people think she chose to commit suicide, rather than blame Othello.

"You heard her words," said Othello. "She's burning in hell now for lying. I killed her; she sinned with Cassio. Ask your husband. He gave me all the proof I needed."

"My husband?" said Emilia, stunned.

"Your husband!" repeated Othello.

"My husband lies to the heart!" screamed Emilia.

"Quiet!" yelled Othello. He threatened Emilia with his sword.

"You don't frighten me!" Emilia answered. Then she screamed, "The Moor murdered my mistress!"

Montano, Gratiano, and Iago hurried into the room. "Iago, if you're a man at all, tell them she wasn't false," demanded Emilia.

"I told Othello what I thought. She and Cassio sinned together," said Iago. "Silence, wife!"

But Emilia's conscience urged her on. "My lady is murdered! And your lies, Iago, caused this crime!"

"Poor Desdemona," said Gratiano. "This marriage proved fatal to you, as it did to your father. If he had not already died of sadness, this news would have led him to suicide."

"She was evil," insisted Othello. "She gave her love to Cassio. And she gave him my token of love."

"The handkerchief!" cried Emilia.

"Silence! Control yourself!" Iago ordered, pointing his sword at her.

Emilia needed to tell the truth. "I found the handkerchief. I gave it to Iago. He'd begged me to steal it."

Othello rushed at Iago, but Montano knocked his weapon from his hand. Iago slipped by, stabbed Emilia, and rushed from the room.

Montano and Gratiano chased him.

"I'm a complete failure," Othello moaned.

"Cruel Moor, she loved you!" gasped Emilia with her final breath.

Othello pulled out another sword he kept in the bedroom. Suddenly, he began to sob. "Oh Desdemona! Dead, dead, oh!" He was still weeping when Lodovico and Montano entered. Officers followed with Iago and Cassio. "Who committed this crime?" Lodovico asked.

"He that was Othello did it," said the Moor. And he ran at Iago a second time, stabbing him. The wound wasn't fatal. "Live!" said Othello with scorn. "To die would be happiness."

Though his scheme was a failure, Iago refused to confess. But evidence of his guilt had been discovered in letters on Roderigo's body.

"You were a great man, Othello. You let yourself be destroyed by one man's schemes," said Lodovico. "What will they say about you now?"

Othello no longer cared. "Say I murdered her for the sake of honor," he answered bitterly.

"Cassio is governor of Cyprus now," Lodovico announced. "Evil Iago deserves torture. And you, Othello, will be our prisoner until Venice decides how to punish you."

"When you write to the Duke, speak of me as I am," Othello said. "I loved well, but not wisely. Jealousy did not come easily, but when it did come, it ruled me completely."

Othello had one final service to perform for Venice; he needed to end the distress he had begun. "Write this down: I once met a Turk who insulted Venice by beating one of her citizens, so I took him by his throat and killed him-- like this!" Pulling out a hidden knife, Othello stabbed himself. He staggered to the bed, and reaching for Desdemona, he sighed. "I kissed you before I killed you. Now, killing myself, I die upon a kiss."

Quietly, Cassio said, "Oh, I feared this. But I thought he had no weapon. What a sad end for a man who was great of heart!"

63

A Guilty Death

COMPREHENSION CHECK

Choose the best answer.

> **Preview Answer:**
> b. kill his wife.

1. Before Othello accuses Desdemona of giving his handkerchief to Cassio, he
   ___a. sends for Cassio.
   ___b. warns Desdemona that she is on her deathbed.
   ___c. forgives Desdemona's crime.
   ___d. tells Desdemona to pray for forgiveness.

2. Othello wants Desdemona's death to be
   ___a. a murder.
   ___b. a suicide.
   ___c. a sacrifice for her sins.
   ___d. an innocent act.

3. Desdemona was "fighting for air" because
   ___a. she was sobbing.
   ___b. Othello was smothering her.
   ___c. her body was limp.
   ___d. Othello pulled the curtains around the bed.

4. Emilia's news of Roderigo's death puzzles Othello because
   ___a. Othello doesn't know Roderigo.
   ___b. Othello expected Iago to be killed.
   ___c. Othello expected Cassio to be killed.
   ___d. Othello threatened Emilia.

5. When Emilia asked, "Who did this to you?" whom did Desdemona blame?
   ___a. Othello
   ___b. Emilia
   ___c. Herself
   ___d. Iago

6. Othello feels threatened by Emilia when
   ___a. Emilia speaks to the dying Desdemona.
   ___b. Emilia says that Iago has lied about Cassio.
   ___c. Emilia pounds on the bedroom door.
   ___d. Emilia won't obey Iago's order to be silent.

7. Brabantio, Desdemona's father, died
   ___a. after Desdemona died.
   ___b. through suicide.
   ___c. from being stabbed.
   ___d. after Desdemona's marriage.

8. Iago killed Emilia because
   ___a. Emilia told the truth.
   ___b. Emilia lied about Iago.
   ___c. Emilia loved Othello.
   ___d. Iago wanted to marry Bianca.

9. Another name for this story could be
   ___a. "Iago, the Failure."
   ___b. "Desdemona's Suicide."
   ___c. "Emilia's Conscience."
   ___d. "A Sad End."

10. This story is mainly about
   ___a. Iago's lies causing Desdemona' death.
   ___b. jealousy destroying Othello's life.
   ___c. Othello forgiving Desdemona.
   ___d. Iago's evil schemes.

Check your answers with the key on page 67.

This page may be reproduced for classroom use.

A Guilty Death

VOCABULARY CHECK

crime	failure	mercy	sacrifice	smother	sob

I. Sentences to Finish
Fill in the blank in each sentence with the correct key word from the box above.

1. Some tribes practiced animal _____ long ago.

2. The engine's _____ to turn off caused the machine to break.

3. Babies can _____ easily if the blankets in their cribs are not well arranged.

4. In this state it is a _____ to drive while drunk.

5. Ian's mother ran to see what was wrong as soon as she heard his loud _____.

6. The soldier showed _____ to his enemy instead of taking revenge.

II. Using the Words
On the lines below, write six of your own sentences using the key words from the box above. Use each word once, drawing a line under the key word.

1. _____

2. _____

3. _____

4. _____

5. _____

6. _____

Check your answers with the key on page 72.

This page may be reproduced for classroom use.

NOTES

COMPREHENSION CHECK ANSWER KEY
Lessons SC 501-1 to SC 501-10

Lesson Number	Question Number										Page Number
	1	2	3	4	5	6	7	8	9	10	
SC 501-1	C	(B)	C	B	A	◇D	B	A	△A	☐B	10
SC 501-2	B	◇D	(A)	C	D	B	D	D	△A	☐D	16
SC 501-3	A	B	◇D	A	(D)	(C)	(C)	D	△B	☐A	22
SC 501-4	◇B	(D)	(D)	C	A	B	D	A	△D	☐A	28
SC 501-5	D	C	D	D	△A	(B)	C	(B)	△C	☐A	34
SC 501-6	C	(D)	◇B	D	(D)	C	A	D	△C	☐B	40
SC 501-7	D	A	(B)	D	◇C	(A)	D	(D)	△C	☐B	46
SC 501-8	B	(B)	◇A	(C)	D	B	(D)	B	△D	☐D	52
SC 501-9	B	(C)	◇D	D	B	(D)	A	(D)	△A	☐D	58
SC 501-10	◇D	C	B	C	C	(B)	D	(A)	△D	☐B	64

○ = Inference (not said straight out, but you know from what is said)

△ = Another name for the story

☐ = Main idea of the story

◇ = Sequence (recalling order of events in the story)

NOTES

VOCABULARY CHECK ANSWER KEY
Lessons SC 501-1 to SC 501-3

1   A PERFECT SOUL   11

    I.
1. purse
2. military
3. evil
4. soul
5. justice
6. bitter

II.

B	J	U	E	K	B	S	S
B	U	E	B	L	L	O	O
V	S	V	B	U	L	U	U
B	T	I	T	I	E	D	L
M	I	L	I	T	A	R	Y
G	C	I	B	T	C	E	S
T	E	U	N	E	E	R	U
D	H	P	U	R	S	E	T

2   WHICH REPORT IS TRUE?   17

    I.
1. witness
2. noble
3. reputation
4. slave
5. confess
6. duke

    II.
1. d
2. e
3. f
4. a
5. c
6. b

3   THE ENEMY IN CYPRUS   23

    I.
1. fleet
2. separate
3. wit
4. value
5. governor
6. kneel

    II.
1. No
2. Yes
3. Yes
4. No
5. No
6. Yes

VOCABULARY CHECK ANSWER KEY
Lessons SC 501-4 to SC 501-6

LESSON NUMBER				PAGE NUMBER

4 HONEST IAGO — 29

I.
1. embarrass
2. pure
3. drunk
4. patience
5. advice
6. generous

5 CHAOS COMES AGAIN — 35

I.
1. monster
2. deny
3. opportunity
4. distress
5. evidence
6. dismiss

II.

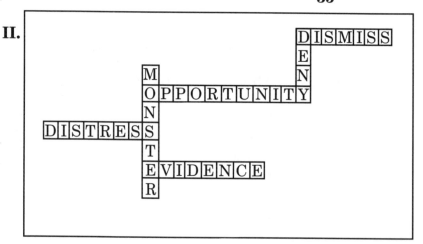

6 THE LOST TOKEN — 41

I.
1. confuse
2. loyal
3. embroider
4. desire
5. visible
6. innocent

II.
1. innocent, e
2. confuse, f
3. loyal, d
4. embroider, a
5. visible, c
6. desire, b

VOCABULARY CHECK ANSWER KEY
Lessons SC 501-7 to SC 501-9

	I.	1. sin	II.	1. d
		2. memory		2. b
		3. plead		3. a
		4. stun		4. e
		5. observe		5. f
		6. civilized		6. c

	I.	1. relative	II.	1. No
		2. behavior		2. Yes
		3. fury		3. Yes
		4. scheme		4. Yes
		5. convince		5. No
		6. obedient		6. No

	I.	1. scorn	II.	1. d
		2. risk		2. b
		3. weapon		3. a
		4. instruct		4. c
		5. thrust		5. a
		6. resolution		6. d

VOCABULARY CHECK ANSWER KEY
Lesson SC 501-10

LESSON NUMBER		PAGE NUMBER
10	A GUILTY DEATH	65

I.
1. sacrifice
2. failure
3. smother
4. crime
5. sob
6. mercy